A HERMIT WITHOUT A PERMIT

by EDDIE DOHERTY

Introduction by Robert Wild

DIMENSION BOOKS
Denville, New Jersey

ISBN 0-87193-005-6

Published by Dimension Books
Denville, New Jersey

Copyright © 1977 by Madonna House

INTRODUCTION

By Father Robert Wild

It was sometime around the beginning of 1975—winter, cold, lots of snow. Father Eddie was playing solitaire in his upstairs portable desert when I came in. "What are the stakes this time?" I asked. "Only two million dollars, not too high," he replied. Two million is *still* pretty high. Father Eddie always played for high stakes.

I sat there for a while in silence, just watching. Father Eddie's presence fostered that kind of posture. He was like the sun in that regard. You didn't have to explain why you had come, and you didn't have to adopt the "right" attitude. You could simply be in his presence and absorb the healing rays that were streaming out of him.

Finally I said: "After you die (we talk quite freely about death in Madonna House) are there any of your writings I can put together in a book for you?" He thought for a moment, then said: "I think there are a couple of books in *Desert Windows*. *Desert Windows* was a series of columns he wrote in our monthly newspaper *Restoration*. I said: "I promise I'll put them together for you." "I'd appreciate that very much," he replied.

"Who should write an Introduction for it?" I asked. He thought for about three seconds and said, "Why don't *you* write it?" A gracious gesture, I thought to myself, but I disregarded it immediately. I was not the one to write such an Introduction. *Desert Windows* might be one of his last books published. I was a newcomer here and had had the privilege of knowing Father Eddie only four years or so. No, it should be written by someone much closer to him. When the time came I would think of somebody.

The time did come, and the more obvious people to introduce his book did occur to me: Catherine, his wife, and Archbishop Joseph Raya, who ordained Eddie into the Melkite rite of the Eastern Church. Thus did *Desert Windows* with these two Introductions come out earlier this year. What I forgot was that there was enough material for two books. This present book is the second. Father Eddie's gracious offer to me is being accepted after all.

To be honest, I have written this Introduction many times in my mind and heart. Even when I really believed I would never write it, composing an Introduction became one of my desert reveries. As I edited his writings, I felt myself coming closer to Father Eddie than I had when he was alive. I entered the workings of his intricate and highly imaginative mind and sometimes felt I knew beforehand what his next sentence or thought-pattern would be. I identified with him so much that, believe it or not, I too began to see windows in my own poustinia! Not simply windows looking onto the forest, but windows like he had—one looking onto the past, one looking onto the Holy Land, and one that's always stuck (that's the one that looks onto heaven). Father Eddie's finally became unstuck on May 4 when he died.

Sometimes at Madonna House, when people used to see Father Eddie and ask who he was, we'd say, "That's Father Eddie Doherty the famous newspaper man who has been married three times. Catherine de Hueck, his third wife, is the foundress of Madonna House. In 1969 Father Eddie was ordained a Catholic priest in Nazareth!"

We'd say it just like that, a whole lifetime packed into a

few sentences without any explanation. Our questioner would smile politely, and we would smile back, the former more confused than before, and we knowing full well he or she thought we were putting him or her on. But it's all true. Father Eddie lost two wives; he will tell you about them in these pages. Then, in 1943, he married Catherine de Hueck who at that time was engaged in her Friendship House Apostolate in Harlem and other cities in the U.S. Eddie has written hundreds of pages about his romance and life with Catherine. I think that his really last book will be the autobiographical account he wrote just before he died. Keep an eye out for it!

As many people now know from Catherine's book *Poustinia,* we have here at Madonna House little hermitages where people can go for a day of prayer and fasting. We call these little cabins *poustinias,* which is the Russian word for desert. When a person goes there for a day, he or she takes along only bread and water, and the only book read there is the Bible. Some of us spend half of the week in the poustinia, emphasizing the prayer and fasting dimensions of our gospel way of life. As I became more familiar with Father Eddie, especially through the manuscript of *Desert Windows,* I really came to see that he was in some deep and profound way the spiritual father of all present and future *poustinikki* here at Madonna House.

Why is this so? Primarily because he was the person closest to the heart of our foundress, Catherine, and he listened to the word of God coming through her with a husband's love, which can never be repeated. Also, because combined in him to a marvelous degree were the virtues of solitude and availability which comprise the distinctive calling of the poustinik.

Solitude? His age and physical condition forced thousands of hours of solitude upon him. He accepted it, entered it more deeply every day, and met there the awesome God of the desert. At the same time he lived in a room that was the crossroads of the world. It was at one and the same time his bedroom, the TV room, a place for meetings and visiting. No one was ever exposed more to the intensity of life of Madonna House than Father Eddie in his portable hermitage.

Poverty? He will joke about the fact that he was forced to travel with only two nurses, a priest, and a personal physician! He will try to throw you off the track with his remarks that he only ate breakfast, lunch, an afternoon snack, supper, and an evening snack—and fasted the rest of the time! Don't let him fool you! Eddie Doherty was the "man about all the towns of the world" who came to live in the tiny village of Combermere, Ontario, in 1947. He was the man who was used to pulling all his own strings and who let go of all of them to allow God to pull them instead.

Chastity? He was married three times! No more need be said about his extremely healthy and robust masculinity. "I still believe," he wrote towards the end of his life, "that God had created nothing more beautiful than a woman." And yet, a few years after their arrival in Combermere, Catherine and Eddie vowed to live apart rather than as husband and wife so as to give to the Lord even the gift of their bodily relationship for the sake of the apostolate. All the desert Fathers were celibate; but I can't recall any one of them leaving a beautiful wife to enter the heart of the desert. Eddie did.

Prayer? Penance? Charity? Well, we'll let Father Eddie tell you himself how the Lord fostered these virtues in him in his desert life. He often called himself "a hermit without a permit" because this venerable hermit traveled every winter to our house in Winslow, Arizona. The Combermere winters were too severe for him. And so he will speak his word from the poustinia now in Winslow, now in Chicago (where he often stopped to visit his family), now in Combermere. As he speaks, don't let his Irish humor blind you to the profound truths the God of the desert burned into his soul. It was his unique way of seeing life which made him bury deep truths amidst puns and imaginative wanderings.

When Father Eddie died I tried to sum up for myself the essence of this view, to sum up how he had achieved such a blending of profound truth and lightness of heart. I decided it was this: he trusted completely his humanity as a way to God. This does not sound like a new idea. But it's a truth which tends to get more and more obscure as one gets "serious" about life with God. Believe me, Father Eddie was serious about his life with God. At the same time, no one was more insistent that everything that God made was very good, and that we could come to God in and through all the gifts of creation. Whether it was humour, food, kissing the girls, the beauties of nature, good times with his friends, Father Eddie never thought of going beyond them to God but somehow *through* them. It was his special grace to be able to do this in a marvelously wholesome way.

We are used to heavy and profound truths about man's life with God appearing in heavy and profound books. The world has many such books. They are among the great treasures of mankind. They nourish our minds and hearts way down deep. But Father Eddie's insights are so well integrated into his view of life that they sneak up on you while he is talking about food or women or rock hunting in

Arizona. Be careful you don't miss them as we often miss the inspirations of God which are woven into our daily humaness. Father Eddie can teach us how to see God amidst the smiles and tears, picnics and deserts of our own lives because he saw Him there.

Alas, his books will never be spiritual classics! Too bad for us! What shall the conversation of heaven be like? Heavy, ponderous, a deep spiritual truth in every sentence? Or will it be light—certainly suffused with truth and beauty—but playful, humorous even? Sometimes, in my more human moments(!), I think that Father Eddie's way of relating to Jesus and Mary and the saints may just possibly be the most natural way of all—the way everybody's doing it now in heaven. And when I think thus I whisper a silent prayer to Father Eddie that he ask the Lord to save me from the wrong kind of seriousness which blocks out grace streaming in through human realities.

So here are the desert meditations of an Irish hermit, descendant of St. Columba's race. You will quickly see that Father Eddie's lifestyle was a bit different from that of his austere predecessor. But we'll have to wait till heaven to see who really loved more.

Robert Wild
Priest of Madonna House

CHAPTER 1

GOD IS A PUSHOVER

"Man is stronger than God," sang the wind.

The silly palm trees shook their plumes in exultation and bent low to the boisterous boasting breeze. "Man is stronger than God," they agreed with a million sibilant whispers. (Palm trees in Canada? No, no, no! Palm trees grow only in the oasis of my Canadian desert—my own private, peculiar, and particular desert. The place is rimmed with palms).

I was reading the Second Book of Kings when the wind began to spread its blasphemy. But was it blasphemy? I tuned into the wind and the dancing palm fronds and the ecstatic wild rose vines and all the bowing and scraping flowers in the garden. I listened more closely and I learned.

Man is stronger than God in the way that a child is stronger than his father. What man—or woman for that matter—will not wake in the night at the cry of a child, slip out of bed and hurry to see what the little one needs? The wail of the baby rules the master bedroom.

Why did St. Paul glory in his weaknesses? Because he knew that he had only to call for help from the Almighty to fill his hands with power.

God has a soft spot. God is a pushover for a prayer. God is the slave of prayer.

Every man has a soft spot too, though it might not be detected in a number of us. We love someone or something inordinately—and we can be badly hurt or even crushed because of this.

Take that wild rose for instance. It shows its love for God in perfume as well as beauty. That's the rose vine's soft spot. A rude hand snaps its pretty head from the stem, raises it to a nose and lets it fall. It may be crushed beneath a clumsy heel. But it has served God's purpose. God made it what it is and put it where it is to please his children and to show his love for them.

He covered the vines with many little thorns. That was his justice. He made the blossoms beautiful and fragrant. That was his soft spot. His love for us. (His soft spot shows in everything on earth!).

"Man is stronger than God," I said in final agreement with the choir-master, the wind and all his enchanting *schola*.

Man, the son of Man, the son of David, the son of Mary, the victim himself, demanded and collected the ransom—amnesty for all the murderers and even an eternal reward for every one of them.

The heavenly Father could have sent those wicked ones to hell—like Lucifer and his satanic army. Instead he forgave them, opened heaven to them, and spread his banqueting table with the choicest foods and drinks.

I rejoiced that I was a man and a priest.

I am weaker than St. Paul yet I am stronger than God! I, too, can summon him with a few words from the highest heaven and he will come immediately into my hands. I can hold him. And I can give him, body and soul, to all who approach the altar.

On the fifteenth of August, 1972, I celebrated the third anniversary of my ordination. I am a priest! I forget that many times. It is incredible that I forget, yet it is more incredible that I am another Christ. I have offered up a thousand masses! And for all I know to the contrary, I may offer a thousand more before I kiss the earth goodbye.

"Our years are as fragile as a spider's web," wrote the Psalmist. "The number of our years is seventy, eighty years perhaps, if we are among the strong."

Sometimes a man wants to be stronger. Sometimes he wishes to be weaker than he is. But always, if he be wise, he lets the Lord decide the measure of the strength he needs. I have had many wild roses on my vines and hardly any thorns. Maybe the vine needs more thorns than blossoms to give true fragrance and beauty to those passing by. Which do I need more? Strength or weakness? Thorns or flowers?

The wind opened one of my windows with a loud and glorious bang and I saw a dusty village close to Mt. Carmel in the Holy Land. I looked closer and saw the Prophet Elisha and his servant Gehazi talking together outside a small but sturdy structure on the flat roof of a house built of stone. I couldn't hear what they were saying, but someone had translated their words into English and put them into the Book of Kings. I had only to lower my eyes.

They were talking about the Shunemite woman who had arranged the bedroom for Elisha when she realized he was a man of God. Elisha wanted to know how he could reward her for her loving care.

"She has no son," Gehazi said. "And her husband is getting on in years."

"Call her," Elisha said to him.

Abruptly the woman appeared. I don't know how she got to the roof. Maybe she climbed a ladder. Maybe she came up through a trap door. She was small and dark and thin and withered. She was half smiling, half suspicious. What could the man of God want of her?

"This time next year," the old man said, caressing his long pepper-and-salt specks of mustard beard, you will be fondling a baby son."

The woman thought he was crazy. Couldn't he see she was too old? Didn't he know that her husband also was too old?

Even God couldn't put a baby in her arms. What led this man to believe himself more powerful than God?

"Yet the woman conceived and by the same time the following year she had given birth to a son as Elisha promised." So said the Book.

Wasn't there something in the gospel of St. Matthew about those who honor a prophet? I turned the pages.

"He who welcomes you welcomes me and he who welcomes me, welcomes him who sent me. He who welcomes a prophet because he bears the name of a prophet receives a prophet's reward."

A prophet's reward! The Shunemite woman had done much for Elisha, giving him a good meal every time he came to the village and finally arranging this room on the roof. Nothing, Elisha thought, would be too good for her. Gehazi's words gave him an idea.

Why not give her a new youth, a new romance, a new honeymoon? Why not let the dead passion of herself bud again and flourish in the wind and sun and the rain of an autumnal love that would far surpass the splendor of its springtime? Why not give both husband and wife another foretaste of heaven?

Maybe this explains the mystery of my priesthood. I always loved priests. I liked to be with them. I like to do things for them. Is that why I was ordained? Was this a reward?

To me it is more than just a priesthood. It is actually an autumnal—no, a winter—romance, a honeymoon that will not fade with the months, that will never wax or wane. If it brings forth "the child" in me, I shall rejoice like the Shumenite.

Elisha's story didn't end with the birth of the boy.

The lad died when he was scarcely old enough to be of help around the house. His mother took the body up to the prophet's room and placed him on the bed. Then she saddled a donkey and went riding up the side of Mt. Carmel.

When Elisha heard the news he sent Gehazi on ahead with instructions to touch the corpse with the prophet's staff. Elisha followed with the mother. Before they reached the house they met Gehazi coming back. He had laid his staff on the boy but he was still dead.

Elisha shut the door of the room after he had entered, leaving the mother outside. I couldn't see him but I heard his voice—I didn't know what he said, but I knew he was praying.

I read from the Book: "Then he lay upon the child on the bed, placing his mouth against the child's mouth, his eyes upon the eyes and his hands upon the hands. As Elisha stretched himself over the child, the body became warm. He arose, paced up and down the room, and then once more lay down upon the boy who now sneezed seven times and opened his eyes."

I tried to open the window that looks on heaven hoping I might see Elisha and ask what sort of prayer he had used. It might "come in handy."

I couldn't budge it. I couldn't even see through it. The pane was frosted on the outside like regular Canadian winters in winter. But the design was different.

It was a mess not of finger prints but of wing prints. Do angels actually wear wings? I doubt it. Anyway, the window wouldn't open.

"It might cost you your life to open that window," a friend remarked not long ago.

"And that would be worthwhile," I said.

"But," said my friend, "how do you know where heaven is—which way to go? Better let your window keep on sticking. Suppose it does not point to heaven?"

However, I thought I knew the sort of prayer the prophet offered. "Lord, after you have restored the soul of this young body, make a child of me even if you have to kill me first. Then put your mouth on mine, your eyes on mine, your hands on mine, and stretch yourself over me. And after I sneeze seven times and open my eyes, stay with me until for the last time I sneeze seven times again."

The prayer in my mind is not much different. "Lord, if you hear me cry out in the night, send your virgin daughter, your virgin spouse, your virgin mother to quiet me and bring me to your arms. Give me the heart of a child and never let me grow too strong, too smart or too sophisticated."

"And please see to it that I get my fair share of the ransom."

CHAPTER 2

THIRTY YEARS IN A CANOE

"How was it?" a friend asked.

"Quiet," I answered. "Nice. Best one so far."

"How do a Catholic priest and his wife celebrate the thirtieth anniversary of their marriage?"

And what I knew he would discern from my answer was that we had spent the day in peace and love—the words engraved into the silver cross of the Madonna House Apostolate.

My friend saw something unique in this. Not many Catholic priests can look back on thirty years of love and peace in marriage. Most of them, begorra, were not married even once (not to mention my three times).

It was a beautiful day, June 25th. It was Monday. A beautiful green Monday with yellow birds singing everywhere around us and squirrels scolding us from the safety of the pines and wild flowers thanking the Lord that at last he had let them see the sun.

I said mass in the old chapel with Father Pelton. I gave Catherine the body and blood of Jesus, son of Mary, son of God. She kissed my hand as though it were the hand of Christ.

Isn't a priest another Christ?

After mass we went to lunch. She had a gift for me. A poem. I had a gift for her—a book I hope to finish before I die. We live in holy poverty. No ropes of diamonds pass from me to her on our anniversary, no fur coats, not even a new Mercedes Benz. She gives me no new yachts, no castles in Spain, no fancy modern apartment buildings. Just thirty years of love in thirty lilting lines.

Afterwards we strolled across the bridge to Hermit Island where she lives. We had a look at the Museum of Religious Arts which she had built last Fall. We spent a few minutes in the great log chapel, "Our Lady of the Woods," and then we went to the poustinia of one of our staff who is on a leave of absence. Catherine poured tea from her samovar as she used to do on festive occasions when we lived in the one-room flat in Chicago.

Afterwards we strolled to the bank of the Madawaska, each carrying a chair that had no weight at all. We sat there a long time talking about nothing much. We were like the stream itself—shallow talk, profound depths in our thoughts.

Catherine was saying something about a canoe that was coming toward us. She liked its grace. She liked its silence. She liked the fact that it didn't frighten the fish or pollute the river.

My eyes, dulled by cataracts—one out, one in—saw only an outline. But it made me think that our marriage was like that.

We hadn't frightened many fish in the last thirty years; we had polluted no particular waters—including those that run under the bridge.

It came to me abruptly that she has been paddling her own canoe for a great many years; and I have been paddling mine. Sometimes we paddle together; sometimes she went upstream and I headed the other way.

"Speaking of canoes," I said, "I just remembered I am celebrating not only our wedding day but also the day Archbishop Raya ordained me a deacon."

"That's the deacon speaking," Catherine said.

It was true. Four years ago on June 25th in the chapel of the Little Sisters of Jesus in Nazareth of Galilee my archbishop gave me the major orders. I was a subdeacon in the morning. I was a deacon in the evening.

I chose the day myself. And I chose Catherine's birthday, August 15th, as the day he was to make me a priest forever and a day. The canoe went by and we were silent again—which is just another way we have of making love. I shouldered my way into my portable desert and tried to open all the windows. It was too stuffy. Two windows stuck. I had no difficulty with the third. But I couldn't see very well. A couple of black olives seemed to be rolling from left to right, then back again. It didn't make sense at all.

I thrust my head through the screen—it was made of cobwebs—and saw a newspaperman trying to brighten up his story. He was wondering which of two lines to use.

Should he say the lady serenaded her ex-lover with the little foreign-made pistol she held in her soft right hand? Or should he say she crocheted him a brand new blood-red shirt by remote control and a seven-gun that sewed with little chunks of lead?

"Why not just say she shot him seven times in the back?" I said, half aloud. Catherine leaned forward as if she wanted to hear what I had muttered but there was a motor boat tearing through the beautiful blue river polluting it savagely and frightening the fish. I shrugged a shoulder toward it saying nothing. Katie understood. Then, a long way behind the boat there was a beautiful young woman standing on a board hanging onto a rope and screaming joyously.

At that moment two people obstructed my view of the

long-legged girl and of the newspaperman and his view of the woman with the singing or crocheting handgun.

One obstructor was a woman who lives "down the road a piece."

"Look at her," this woman said. "She ain't got on enough clothes to cover a gooseberry." That was, of course, a great exaggeration.

The other obstruction was a very young and holy seminarian. He was looking at a young lady who was dressed something like our waterskier and there was rapture in his eyes. "Look at her," he shouted. "Isn't she one of the most beautiful things God ever made? Oh, thank God for beauty like that."

The seminarian, as a grand old poet once expressed it, "told the sexton and the sexton tolled the bell." The rector of the seminary was also going to toll the bell. But he didn't. He let the young idealist become a priest and later on, a wonderful archbishop.

Before I returned to my desert window I asked myself a question. How was it that my eyes could see only the outline of the canoe, and that dimly, whereas I could see the girl clearly? The answer was simple. The sun must have been wiping its face with a cloud when the canoe went by; and it must have dropped the cloud in a hurry so it too could see the girl.

I thanked God for the girl and for Catherine too. I thanked him most especially for Catherine; and went right back to the wide open window of my collapsible desert to see the newspaperman listening to a friendly priest. I overheard every word he said.

"At one time he was a good Catholic boy. He told me that himself. He was never going into politics, he might lose his faith. A lot of Ku-Kluxers in politics in this part of Indiana. How he got involved with the woman, I don't know. But he told me and he told her too that he would never marry her because she was a divorcee. Good Catholic men never marry divorced women. So what does he do but marry another divorcee. And there you are.

"He was standing on his back porch when the first divorcee stepped into the yard below him. He saw her and deliberately turned his back on her, which of course, he never should have done. It gave her a target she otherwise wouldn't have had. The lady opened her handbag and sent seven lead congratulations to the bridegroom. Her object was evil but her aim was good.

"I got to the house a few moments later to hear the dying man's confession. He swore at me. He threatened me. He went into such a frenzy that I was asked to leave. I came back later determined to save his soul in spite of him. He cursed me again and raised such a racket the doctors and nurses almost threw me out. So I went back a third time. And for the third time I was driven out of his sight. God have mercy on him. Maybe, at the very last moment, he may have repented. The mercy of God is so infinite! Even at the last second a man can be saved by asking God for mercy."

I shut the window softly. What had all this to do with Catherine and me?

I shut it but I sneaked back every little while and opened it. And things began to clear up in my mind.

I was covering the trial and a friend in the office of the *Chicago Sun* was sending Catherine's letters to me. She was running Friendship House in New York and writing me letters everyday to say she would never, never, never marry me. I never answered them. If you want a woman to go on saying "no," write her every morning, noon and night. If you want her to say "yes," ignore her.

Early in the trial I wrote about the widow. She came to court every day and sat quietly in her chair never moving hands or feet but perpetually rolling her black eyes—"like ripe olives on a clean white plate."

A few days later my friend forwarded me a letter from Catherine demanding to know who the woman was who rolled her beautiful black eyes at me. Was she really so lovely as I thought?

I had an impulse to ask the *Sun* to replace me at the trial and to catch the first plane leaving Indiana for New York. But nobly and wisely I put seven little leaden slugs in the idea's back.

"Kid," I announced, "Spring's in the air. Keep writing about the beauty of other women, each and every one who comes into the news. Soon you can pick enough wild flowers to make a big bouquet for your June bride."

I began to say nice things about the woman on trial. I felt I owed her something. Maybe I did at that. I began to feel a sneaking likeness for her too. I asked Blessed Martin, my great pal, to help her.

What did Martin do? He put a light-colored black on the jury. And what did I do? I bet a lot of people that the woman would never be convicted, would never be sent to state prison. What happened? The jury disagreed. The lady was never tried again. She was held in the local jail a few months and then released.

A bell rang. Catherine and I went to vespers in the big log chapel, then had dinner served us in the poustinia. A dinner superbly cooked! We really do have the best cooks in Madonna House—the best east of the Pacific and west of the Atlantic.

And we have the best strawberries ever grown. The girls picked more than 500 pounds of berries in two days; some were as big as golf balls. (And better tasting).

Strawberries and ice cream. And no black olives on my plate.

The glorious day was done; another thirty years of nuptial bliss stretched out its arms to us.

So, kind friends, take my advice: always live in love and peace, and don't go frightening other people's fish.

CHAPTER 3

THE MOST UNMORTIFIED CHRISTIAN

Today, outside my private desert oasis of Combermere, a beautiful young woman uncameled her weary self and came despondently into my cell. "I am in a very bad mood," she said. "Tell me a joke or two."

"I never saw you in a bad mood before," I said. "What is the matter?"

"I guess it goes back to the days when I was a nun," she said. "I was a nun for a year or more. It was the most horrible experience in my life. Twice I wanted to kill myself I was so wretched."

"How could you be a nun," I asked, "and feel like that! I thought all nuns were happy."

"It was this business of mortifying the eyes. We were told, 'If you see a tree and you know it's beautiful don't look at it. If you see a flower pretend not to look, look away from it. If you hear a bird singing do not look and do not listen. If you look up at the stars at night shut your eyes quickly and shut out heaven.' "

Lord, how can anyone know you who is not allowed to look at you?

I marvelled that my caller had been able to stand this moritification for a year or more.

"But," she said, "I was one of the very few who left the order. The other nuns are still there, still mortifying themselves, so there must be something holy in this self-martyrdom."

A long time after she had left I kept staring out of the window of my past, thinking of all the times I rejoiced at seeing you, Lord, and all the beauties you have shown me throughout my crazy life.

The more often I see you, the more clearly I see you. The more often I see you, the closer I come to you. If I ignored you, how can I adore you?

If I should go blind tomorrow I will still remember a thousand beauties you have set before my eyes.

I saw through the window acres and acres of pink and white and red carnations, bobbing and bowing in the breeze and filling the world with the spicy fragrance of their breath.

I was six or seven years old, and that is more than seventy-five years ago, but I can still see the flowers you made and smell the aroma you put into them. The color and movements you gave them; and so I remember you.

So I see you; and seeing you, I love you!

Somehow or other I see you best in flowers. A water lily floating in a swamp. A country lane bordered on both sides by Queen Anne's lace. A stately row of hollyhocks and sunflowers and fire-blue shafts of larkspur peering at me from over the top of a friendly fence and giving me your regards. A bit of edelweiss ambushed on a cloud-veiled, shining mountain peak. A humble blue flower looking at me from a prairie in Wisconsin as a narrow gauge train stopped for a few minutes at a rustic station.

I wanted to leap off the train and pick that flower. I have been sorry ever since that I didn't do it. I didn't know then that it was a love letter from you, but I know it now. A letter I have read again and again although I never opened its envelope.

I awoke one night in a plane high over the Atlantic and looked down, half asleep, to see the ocean of fire!

I was astounded for a moment at such a miracle. How could the ocean burn? The whole wide ocean! I kept looking at it in awe. I saw the red flames leaping up everywhere to fall back on the surface in golden splendor. Then, only then, I realized that what I saw, O Maker of millions and billions of seas and suns, was merely a reflection of the rising sun—and that the plane would soon land prosaically and yet exultantly, thanks to you, in the airport of Amsterdam.

That sea of fire still surges in me at times, brightens my life, and makes me cry out your name.

Perhaps some people can see you better than I do through mortifying their eyes. Many people do love you more than I do but I love you not only with my eyes but with all my senses and all my crazy heart. I forget you hours at a time. I do not think of you. I do not feel your presence. The joy of being with you is not mine. I am busy about many things.

Yet, all the time I know you have not forgotten me!

I thank you, Lord, for all the wondrous things that have happened to me through your benevolence and mercy.

And, while I think of it, let me specially thank you and your lovely mother for the Seven Dolors Rosary my brother Martin left me.

Martin was a priest for more than forty years in the diocese of Portland, Oregon. When he died last November, the rosary came to me a few weeks later.

Marty, a year or so before he died, wrote an account of the progress made by the Servite Order in Oregon. The Servites inducted him into their Order. He wore the habit and the rosary. Now the rosary is mine.

You remember, Lord and Lady, how happy I was when the first Seven Dolors rosary was given me in the Servite Monastery in Granville, Wisconsin. You remember I wore it proudly for about as long as Martin wore his. For a year or so—the time the young woman spent in her convent.

I was about fourteen at that time. Later I decided the priesthood was not for me. I left the monastery. I became a newspaperman. I married Marie. I married Mildred. I married Catherine. Then in 1969 I became a priest.

After nearly seventy years you gave me back the rosary of Our Lady of Sorrows! It is one of my greatest treasures.

I was praying the other night, rolling the beads through my fingers, when I saw Mary and Joseph start off to Jerusalem to look for Jesus who was then about twelve or thirteen.

They searched for three days before they found him in the temple talking to the priests and the elders.

And you, Lord, inspired me to stop them and to ask them if they would not also look for some friends of mine among the living and the dead, friends who have been lost, some for many years.

"You don't have to look far for them now," I said. "You will not look for them in the temple. You know exactly where they are for God has given you great power. He made you both custodians and caretakers of his friends. All the people of the world are his friends, especially the lost ones who need him so sorely. Please bring them back with you to Nazareth where they belong."

I thank you also for sending me every year to the Madonna House in Winslow, Arizona, to the new chapel where I have said so many masses and where I have gathered so many friends.

I thank you for the grey-green hills beyond the city limits which abound in pieces of petrified wood—"real Arizona jade."

I thank you for sending Catherine and Father Briere there last February to help me pick up some of that petrified wood and to bless my little congregation with their presence.

When it comes to eyes, ears, nose, taste, and touch, I am probably the most unmortified Christian in the whole wide world. I like it that way.

I have a window in my desert, as you know, which looks up toward heaven. It always sticks. I cannot open it. I have come to the conclusion that this doesn't matter.

I have seen you here on earth again and again and again. And I am sure, somehow in spite of myself, I shall see you face to face in heaven.

Why do I need a window when I can look at you with my eyes?

But Lord, be kind. Let your queen be present when we meet. She will give me the courage to stand before you and to lift my eyes to you.

CHAPTER 4

MYSTIC MAGIC OF THE ROSARY

There must be some mystic magic in the rosary sent me by Our Lady of Sorrows through the death of my brother Martin.

It seems to give me a wider vision, a deeper look into certain events in Our Lady's life.

The other day, with her beads in my hand, I was looking at her as she stood on Calvary beneath the cross of her son.

Jesus was nailed to that wood, his arms outstretched as far as he could reach—far enough to embrace the whole world. His knees were raised and one foot rested on the other—a great spike running through each, holding them fast. There was a crown of thorns on his head. There were tears in his eyes and on his cheeks there was a light of glory and triumph and great joy on his face.

I looked at Mary and saw that her eyes were shining with love and admiration and adoration. Reflecting the light in the eyes of her son. And then the picture began to recede and I went forward somehow in time and space. Or should I say I went backward?

I found myself some place in Egypt. I knew it was Egypt because in the background I could see the pyramids and the Sphynx, those man-traps designed to catch and hold eternity, the immortality, the everlasting life and richness of the gods!

Mary was still looking at her son. He was a baby. He lay naked on a little wooden table outside the house. Mary had just bathed him and he was lying with his arms outstretched as though the world were not too wide for him to hold and fondle. His knees were drawn up and one foot rested on the other. There was a crown of lights and shadows on his silky head and glory and adoration in his eyes.

Joseph, his foster-father, stood by silent for a long time. A tall, strong young man, black hair and just a little red in his beard, mighty hands and great wide shoulders. There was adoration in his eyes too.

He spoke gently to Mary, making a gesture towards the child.

"Like a lamb come up from the washing," he said, remembering a line from the psalm written by one of his ancestors.

A look of anguish came into Mary's face but did not change the look of joy and adoration and glory.

She had forgotten about the lamb until this moment. She had forgotten the words of Simeon which let her know that this child was a sign of contradiction who would be sacrificed for Israel and for the Gentiles.

She had forgotten his prophecy that a sword would pierce her own heart.

She had been too happy in holding her son to her breasts and letting him drink his fill. It was glorious to know that she, an ordinary, humble woman could not only give life to God but also maintain him with her milk.

She was happy to see him at play. She was happy to look at him every night as he slept in the crib Joseph had so cleverly made for him.

To be with God constantly, to know God, to love him and to adore him, and to be loved and needed by him—what woman could know more joy than that?

But Joseph's words brought back the memory of that

Passover when the blood of a lamb was sprinkled on the doors by the Hebrews so that the Angel of Death would not visit their homes.

That night the first-born son of every Gentile family in Egypt died in his sleep; and Pharaoh let Moses take the Jews toward their promised land.

That was a long, long time ago. Now it was the son of God whose blood would be sprinkled on the doors of all his followers so that the angel of death—eternal death—would pass them by!

This child lying so sweetly before her, his eyes lighted with love and benediction, this lamb of God would be lifted up some day. And he would hang on the cross in just that way, his knees raised, his arms strung out from side to side (and fastened tightly), a crown of thorns biting into his head.

When would it happen?

She would have to wait. Maybe it would take years, many years. Only he and his Father knew when and where he would be slain.

I saw this plainly through the window that looks out on Judea and Galilee and Egypt and all the places where the Son of Man has walked and I could not sleep.

Last January I bought a belt on which to hang this rosary. I wanted to wear it as I wore it when I was a boy in the Servite Monastery in Wisconsin. But the belt was too wide for the loops on my trousers. And carrying a rosary is impractical in hunting petrified wood. So I abandoned this belt and I keep the rosary under my pillow.

I went to Toronto recently and made an appointment with Dr. Callahan in St. Michael's Hospital. Later, Father Briere and I visited my cancer clinic in Ottawa.

I have been a faithful and loyal patient at this clinic for many years—ever since one of their doctors took a skin-cancer out of my nose.

At their request I have visited the clinic at least once a year in all kinds of weather—rain, shine, sleet and snow.

So can you imagine my anguish, my horror, my frustration, my dejection, my shame, my humiliation and my Irish anger when I was told that I was no longer welcome, no longer a member in good standing?

One of the doctors said, not in so many words, but in essence,—"You are a phony, you are a fake, you are a fraud, you are an impostor. You never had cancer and you never will. Get out of here this minute and never show your face in this holy place again. You are cured! You are ended! You are done."

I came home to my oasis in Combermere disheartened, woeful, dejected, rejected, unwanted, abandoned, forsaken, all on my own from now on—only to be embraced by my dear Old Aunt Jina Pectoris. A collection of doctors refer to her, solemnly and sometimes timidly, as angina pectoris. But she's been in the family so long and she comes to visit me so often—especially in humid or "muggy" weather, that we have taken her into the family as some sort of relative. The rubber iceberg I wear at times over my heart numbs the pressure of her wicked knee.

She put her bony arms around me and hugged herself to my aching bosom!

There is balm in Gilead. I have at least one friend who is attached to me for life—my life.

Just had a great inspiration. Why don't I teach the Old Girl to say the rosary with me? Both the Dominican Rosary and that of Our Lady of the Seven Sorrows.

If her fingers are busy with the beads they won't press so heavily into my chest.

Many people have asked: "Why don't you pray to Our Lady or to your friends, St. Martin de Porres and the Little Flower, to drive 'Aunt Jina' away from you and keep her away?"

All I could answer was the bit of wisdom given me by a holy priest not so long ago. "My mother used to say," he said, "Never pray hard for anything you particularly want, you might get it."

If God wants to chase the old girl away, let him do it. If he doesn't want to, let her hang around. I'm getting used to her anyway. Maybe some day we'll get married—that is—God forbid—if a man can marry his aunt!

CHAPTER 5

VOICE OF THE FATTED CALF

The sun, the lion of the dawn, was eating the last of the night's carcass and making a gory mess of it when I arose that beautiful October morn. He had no napkin around his red neck so he nuzzled and muzzled the sky. And look at it!

You thought the heart's blood of the night was black? You see now it is a glorious shade of red. I guess all blood is red.

Heat waves were dancing like a thousand strippers over the miles and miles of sand. My desert was empty or so I thought. At least I could see no one. I was gazing through the window that opens on the footprints I made on my way to this oasis. The Lord had covered them with sand but they were still there. I could see them well.

And something or someone was out there, mooing at me. Actually mooing. A cow calling a calf? A calf calling a cow? Ridiculous! Impossible! This part of the desert was un-cowed.

"Mooooooooooooooooo!"

That voice, I thought, should have come through the window that looks on heaven since it is a voice not meant for ears. I was tempted to try opening that window. But I resisted. That's the one that's always coated with frost or fog or heavy snow. That's the one that always sticks.

I said mass and went to dinner. One of the priests read aloud after the blessing. But all I heard was the call of a cow or a calf. If it were some kind of code, I couldn't read it. Maybe I should walk around and not try to think of anything; walk around the house and garden and just listen. I went outside and walked.

All I heard was the chatter and patter from a chain of pretty girls. It stretched from the dining room through the kitchen across the porch and over the lawn as far as St. Clare's cabin. The girls moving books from one place to another.

"Only detective fiction," one of the girls said, passing four or five books to the next in line who passed them on. "Our library can't be confined to the dining room. It has to spread. We're just moving part of it!"

"Mooing?"

She thought that was funny for no reason at all.

"Moving," she said in the tone of a pretty girl used to correcting a venerable and holy priest.

I went to my room to my neglected typewriter. Another pretty girl came waltzing in. "It's a glorious day," she said. "I've come to take you for a ride."

We traveled for miles watching the October parade of the trees. I don't know any other place in the world where one can see such autumn colors as in this region around Madonna House in Combermere.

We went slowly. Every tree was a prayer. And every prayer we said was a tree standing straight before the Lord to give him thanks for all this loveliness. There was one tall maple tree from which the red leaves fell like blood from the cross. And it talked to me. It said the one word, "mooooooooooo!"

Slowly I began to uncode the message. First I deciphered the name of the sender. Father Joe Ferguson. He was the pastor of the church in Warkworth, Ontario when he died.

I had heard of him long before I met him. Catherine used

to talk about him and about the stories he told the kids in her first Friendship House in Toronto.

He used to come in every once in a while, she said, with half a cow over his strong right shoulder—enough meat for all the staff and all the men who came to the place for food and warmth and comfort—and for friendship, too. That Friendship House was opened on October 15th, 1930. Did the date have anything to do with the "moo?" Who knows?

I wondered a long time about that after returning from the ride. I decided that it did not. And I was sure it had something to do with this crazy call of the cow. But how? Of course! His cousin Pat!

"I went to visit St. Anne's shrine one year," Father Ferguson told me, "and met a relative of mine. To my great surprise I discovered he was a validly ordained priest. He didn't know a word of Latin. He could hardly speak a word of English. But he was a priest! He gave me a marvelous account of how that came to be. He was working on a farm when quite suddenly he felt God wanted him to be a priest. He threw down his pitchfork and went to see the farmer. 'I'm lavin yez,' he said. 'I got the call.'

'You got what?' the dumbfounded farmer asked.

'The call. The call to the praisthood.'

'Arra go on with you. 'Tis the cow callin' her calf you heard. Get back to your manure.'

"But my bold laddybuck put on his hat and coat, thrust his shaving kit and his other shirt into a paper bag, and walked to the Jesuit monastery nineteen miles away. The Jesuits couldn't take him. No order would take him. He walked to Detroit and found a job as janitor in a little church. He kept insisting to the pastor that he had the call.

"The pastor tried to help him. He tried to teach Paddy

Latin; but my poor cousin couldn't even say *'Dominus tecum.'* Be that as it may, a bishop from out West stopped in Detroit on his way to St. Anne's shrine and he dropped in to see Paddy's pastor, an old friend.

"The bishop was desperate for priests and the pastor introduced him to Paddy—after confiding the fact that the lad would never take a prize for brilliance but that there wasn't a holier Irishman in the world. The bishop said, 'Bedad, Dakota didn't need brilliant priests, but it certainly needed the holy kind.'

'I'll decide the matter,' he said, 'when I come back from the shrine!'

"He came back with his mind made up. Maybe St. Anne had whispered a word or two in Pat's favor.

"And there was the boyo himself. A farmer dressed up like a priest, his eyes shining with holy joy, telling me it wasn't a cow's moo at all but a real true call from the Lord himself and his Blessed Mother and his Grandmother!"

I wasn't quite convinced that I had solved the bovine cypher. Maybe "Flewy," Grace Flewelling, also had something to do with it. She and Father Ferguson were great friends in life. They were probably in heaven still praying for the holy souls.

Flewy was fond of mooing and then telling everybody, "I'm the cow's tail, always hanging behind."

Surely there must be something more than this—if it were really a message from the throne.

"Mooooooooooo!"

This time the voice seemed to come from the "heaven window." And this time I knew what it was. It was the voice of the fatted calf in the parable Jesus told—the fatted calf that was going to be butchered and served to the prodigal son when he returned, repentant to his father's house—the fatted calf that welcomed all the people to the banquet in the sinner's honor. All day that calf had been trying to find the right stable in my so-called brain. Now he had made it. "You too are invited to be a fatted calf," his message fully decoded said. "You are invited to the banquet of the Lord so that prodigal sons and daughters can dine on you, know they are forgiven all their sins, and realize they are welcome forever in their father's home."

I thought that over for awhile.

Jesus when he related that parable must have been thinking of his own father, the Lord God Almighty, and of the banquet being prepared in heaven for the prodigals on earth.

His father wasn't fattening a calf for them. He wasn't going to butcher a lamb. He was going to give his guests the divine body and blood of his only son! Jesus is called "the lamb of God." And many of us think of him as such. But he was and is a man. He was and is God.

He was and is ordained to be the food of men, all men, saints as well as sinners.

I moved a step—just one step—closer to the window and answered the fatted calf in the same code, "mooooooooooo! mooooooooooo! mooooooooooo!"

That means, "Roger, Wilco; O.K. Say Hi to Flewy and Father Joe and all my people in purgatory and in heaven. They can nibble on me too if they need to."

CHAPTER 6

WALTER WINCHELL IS DEAD

Peace on earth! My old friend Walter Winchell has found peace beyond the earth. I was saddened at the news of his death and his unattended burial. Yet that did not dim the glory of the day, the clear bachelor-button skies (Walter's daughter, the only one at the funeral besides the undertaker and Rabbi, put bachelor-buttons on his coffin. They were, she said, his favorite flowers). Surely a man who arranges to be buried with the rites of his church is not very far from God, "the resurrection and the life." If a man's grave be blessed, may not there be a blessed plot reserved for him high above the graveyard?

One of my three desert windows opened. The one that covers my past. I saw Winchell and Mark Hellinger at a table in Larry Fay's most spacious speakeasy in Manhattan; I was with them paying more attention to their odd conversation than to anybody else or anything else around me including the blond Texas Guinan and her loud greeting, "Hello Sucker!" to every incoming customer, drunk or sober.

This was the summer or fall of 1924. I had come to New York from Hollywood. Phil Payne, managing editor of the *New York Daily News,* a great friend, made me something of a "Broadway big shot." I didn't know anything about the street. I didn't know anything about its people. But I had the luck, or maybe bad luck, to throw a famous comedian down a flight of steps on my first night in the Broadway district and that established me as some sort of expert on the life and morals of old Broadway.

Payne knew everything and everybody. He dug up many stories and I wrote them under my by-line. Hence my reputation grew.

Mark Hellinger was on the *Daily News* when I came, but sometime afterwards he went to work for the *Daily Mirror*. Winchell was the star of the *Graphic*, a new paper competing not too well with the *Mirror* and the *News*. The three of us naturally got together. And together each night we visited the nightclubs. I wanted news. Mark and Walter wanted gossip.

I hated the job. It was to me the essence of sterility. I sat at some sloppy table for an hour or two drinking bootleg whiskey, tipping sloppy waiters, watching millionaires turn into clowns and women into sots, wishing I were home with my wife Mildred and my two boys Eddie, Jr. and Jack Jim. Often, drunken men or women would crawl or stagger or reel up to the table and give some news to Walter or Mark. But mostly the three of us just sat there hour after hour, in one nightclub or another, and Mark and Walter made up a new kind of language. They used such new phrases as "middle-aisling it" and "making whoopee" and having a "blessed event." They didn't smile as they talked. They never laughed. They were almost grim in their seriousness. It wasn't art the way they labored for their effects; it was business. It often made me remember Jack Lait, the great Chicago writer who "would rather coin a new phrase than eat an apple."

I liked Winchell and I liked Hellinger but I felt they were wasting their lives. Neither would ever amount to anything. I was glad when Payne took me off the Broadway beat.

I saw my friends frequently in the years that followed.

Yesterday's open window brought them back vividly. I saw Walter's face distorted with anger. He had written a few lines in his column that made me laugh and that also annoyed me. In his new kind of language he said "Mildred Doherty is in the Larchmont Hosp. for an appen op."

"What's the matter?" he shouted when I found him. "Didn't you like my squib?" I guess he was always angry when people didn't like his stuff. "It was nice of you, Walter," I said, "to think of her but you got everything all wrong. There is no hospital in Larchmont and there was no operation for appendicitis. She is in the New Rochelle hospital minus a tumor."

"Oh," he said, anger gone. "Maybe I should have checked. She all right?"

I saw him again, not in the *Graphic* office but in his cluttered doll house in the *Daily Mirror* building. I brought a friend with me who wanted to meet the great celebrity.

"Mr. Winchell," the boy introduced himself, "I'm known as the black Walter Winchell of Harlem." Winchell rose from his chair and extended his hand. "And I," he said "am the black Walter Winchell of the United States, Canada, and all the ships at sea."

His daughter said he died of a broken heart. Maybe he did. He always felt that every man and woman in his column was an enemy at heart, that he had no friends. Maybe he died of loneliness. I think that's what killed Mark Hellinger too. Sheer loneliness.

There is a vague story about Mark which I never tried to verify. He is said to have bet something like $60,000 at odds of ten to one on Jim Braddock, an old and forgotten boxer who had miraculously arranged to fight the great Maxie Baer, the champion of the world. He won. And, so the legend goes, Mark collected more than half a million dollars and went immediately to Hollywood where he bought a producership and became a movie magnate—a cellophane mogul.

I saw him once on the set during a visit to Hollywood. He invited me to dine with him. We walked through many sets until we entered a tremendous dining room. We were the only ones there and there was only one waiter to serve us though it was the middle of the day. Mark explained, knowing he didn't have to, "Eddie, you know how it is. Scenario writers eat only with scenario writers, actors eat only with other actors, directors eat only with other directors. Producers eat only with producers. There are very few producers so I usually eat alone."

He offered me a job. "I got a story in mind for you. Write it for me and I'll make you a fortune. Take a husband and wife on their fiftieth wedding anniversary, the children and grandchildren and all the guests have gone. They are sitting alone by the fire. He says to her, 'I wonder what would have happened if I hadn't collided with you that April day. Remember how you came around the corner, the wind blowing you and you rushed right into my arms all rosy and red and excited and lovely?' They pass out of each other's lives. Now you carry on from there."

When I was leaving him he asked if I would like to be a war correspondent. He said he could fix it for me with King Features. "The job will pay a lot of money," he said. "Errol Flynn, the great heroic ham of the movies wanted it. He thought it would be great publicity for him, but when he learned that the job was available only because a correspondent had been killed in action he abruptly didn't want it."

"I don't know," I said. "I just came home from covering the beginning of the war. And right now I'm fighting a war of my own more important to me than any war in Europe. It's a war with a blue-eyed Russian blonde who can say no in eighteen languages and mean it every time. If I can get her to say yes to me, I'll say yes to you."

The window slammed shut as Mark turned to go to his office. Almost immediately it opened again to let me see Phil Payne once more. He was showing me through the plane which he intended to fly across the Atlantic. These were the days before Lindbergh made the crossing simple. I closed the window hurriedly.

I still remember how I felt when I read that pieces of the plane were found floating hundreds of miles off the coast of Newfoundland. I was glad the window had opened though, for Payne was still smiling when I wished him bon voyage so many, many years ago.

I spent a long, long moment there in the desert yesterday looking at the window I had closed. Then I tried to open the window that looks on heaven. Alas, it is still stubborn.

I wanted to get a little closer to the Lord so I could put in a good word for Winchell and for Mark and for Phil Payne and for the newspapermen and newspaperwomen I knew. Especially those who have lived beyond their time. I wanted to pray for all the newspapermen and women, the living and dead, and I wanted to give thanks that I am still a newspaperman and one of the happiest on earth.

Also, I wanted to ask God to strengthen my faith so that I may believe he will actually give us a lasting peace if I ask him to. I wanted to say I was willing to give my life for peace in the world as he did. But after all, who wouldn't die for such a peace? Only a few years ago—in 1917—hundreds of American boys were eager to go to war, in "a war to end all wars," and to die for peace if they had to.

It was crazy, of course, to think we could find peace by going to war. I remember a drill sergeant in one of the camps I visited shouting to a bunch of rookies, "jab them bayonets deep into his guts. What's the matter? Do you love that damn dummy? Can't you see he's a Hun? You hate him! Jab that knife deeper—jab it, do you hear me—jab it!"

The only thing that will bring world peace is world love. Only love is stronger than hate. Let us teach all our children not to hate, but to love. Then we may have peace forever, here and hereafter.

This is indeed an extremely happy day. A sunrise of peace appearing in the Eastern skies. "Let the rivers clap their hands, and the mountains shout for joy. Glory to God in the highest and on earth peace, good will to men." Tomorrow may be gloomy, but thank God for today.

CHAPTER 7

DO TEARS REDEEM?

Of all the weird and wondrous deserts inside or outside of the house, the oddest I think is that of our Madonna House here in Winslow, Arizona.

Can you imagine anything more weird and wonderful than waking from a dream, then lying wide awake all the rest of the night while a soundless voice spellbinds you with a story stranger than a dream?

This happened to me sometime ago—and I still know sleepless nights. This voice didn't come through the heaven-pointing window, the one that always sticks. It came from behind my left shoulder. It came into my mind, not through my ears, but from somewhere between them.

Pretend I am the voice talking solemnly and slowly. Ready? Here goes!

"At first Father Oculist tried to excuse his way through the overcrowded aisle that led to the right of the stage. He made no progress, neither with elbow or shoulder nor with 'so sorry,' or 'excuse please.' He took another tack. 'Make way for the cardinal, please.' Men and women stepped aside and he weaseled by. He was afraid he might be too late. That would be Father Jeweler's fault. Father had suggested he come through the audience. 'If Father Pat sees you sitting on the stage with all the big shots,' he had explained, 'he'll know something's up. The Irish sense things. Through their pet leprechauns, I guess.' It was essential that Father Oculist get to the stage quickly for Father Pat was finishing his speech. He must get there in time to present the magnificent farewell gift.

"He was still trying to make progress when the Right Reverend Monsignor Finnegan saw him and guessed his purpose. 'Let that priest through,' he ordered.

"Men and women melted away on both sides even as the Red Sea waters parted to let the Israelites through.

" 'When I told my staff I was forced to resign as head of this great university on account of my eyes,' Father Pat said, 'I told them sternly there was to be no formal farewell reception, no goodbye banquet, and no gold watch to be awarded me for faithful service and good conduct.'

" 'I saw a man paid off that way once, a long time ago. He had never missed a work day in fifty years. Now he was old and slow and rather useless. So they retired him and gave him a gold watch! A twenty dollar gold watch for fifty years of hard labor!

" 'And you see what happened! Here you are. Four or five thousand of you. Maybe more. And people preparing a banquet. And I have a strong suspicion that Father Oculist is bringing me my watch! Well, it's human nature. If you hate or fear your boss you obey him. That's wisdom. But if the old man is the fatherly type you disobey him knowing he'll forgive you.'

"By this time Father Oculist had won his way through the crowd and was standing head bowed before his superior, the gift clutched tightly but not too tightly in his right hand.

" 'The watch,' Father Pat said. 'Hold it high, Father Oculist, so the people can see it.' He seized the priest's wrist and lifted the arm high. The priest struggled.

" 'Be careful, Father Pat,' he said. 'This is something more than a watch. You might break it.'

"It was indeed much more than a watch. It was the most beautiful reading glass Father Oculist has ever made and it would be a great blessing for a man with such poor eyes as Father Pat's. It would be indispensable for the research awaiting him. Father Oculist had twice fitted Father Pat with glasses. He knew exactly how to grind the miraculous lens. He used thick glass and glass so fragile a kiss might shatter it.

"Father Jeweler had seen him at work and had inspired the whole university to help. A Japanese artist carved a delicate ribbon of ivory to hold the glass. Half a dozen sculptors etched liturgical symbols into this and reproductions of several ikons Father Pat loved. One had had the kindness to bless it with a wee shamrock.

"The student body bought a perfect diamond, something over four and a half carats. And two of the trustees donated smaller diamonds, one to be set on either side of the big one.

"Father Oculist had worked on the gift two or three hours every night for the last four months. Many times as he worked he listened to one or another of Father Pat's tapes. It seemed to help him. He had a heroic admiration for the man and for his glorious voice. He liked the frequent flashes of Finnegan wit. He liked most his sermons and homilies. But he didn't like his irony, his sarcasm nor his belittlement of other theologians. With a few words Father Pat could make some fellow writer's profundities sound like the drivel of a retarded imbecile. Was that fair? There was love in everything Father Pat said or wrote. But there was only ice in Father Pat.

" 'Higher,' Father Pat shouted, almost lifting Father Oculist off the floor. He was doing it playfully with comic benevolence but Father Oculist was still struggling. And he was getting angry.

"Suddenly Father Pat covered the priest's little right hand with his big one and squeezed it—laughing as he did so. Anything for a laugh!

" 'Maybe it isn't a watch Father Oculist has,' he confided to the delighted audience. 'Maybe it's only a lemon. Who'd like some lemonade?'

"He squeezed a trifle harder. And something broke! Then something snapped! Then something cracked!

"Was Father Pat breaking every bone in the little priest's hand?

"Apparently Father Pat thought so for he let go his grip and stepped back a little. 'Your hand is bleeding, Dave,' he said, his face softening a little, the wide smile disappearing.

"Father Oculist opened his hand and gazed at all it held. He wished he could drop dead. Father Pat's powerful fingers had brought those three perfect diamonds into collision, and the three little ones had cleaved their priceless mother in three unequal parts as neatly as a lapidary's chisel could have done it. One of the leather wings had been torn off. The ivory rim had been shattered and scratched. And the glass itself was smashed.

" 'Your lemonade, Father,' he said, pouring the rubble into his hands. 'I'm sorry. But you asked for it, didn't you?'

"The great orator said nothing. His face had hardened again.

" 'You're a hard man, Father Pat!' Fr. Oculist remarked. He spoke softly but everybody in that vast assembly hall could hear him. He was speaking close to the mike. 'You are hard on yourself, God knows. You are harder on your enemies. You are hardest on your friends!'

" 'Let Father Surgeon look at your hand,' Father Pat said. 'You seem to have slivers of glass in it.'

Looking into the old priest's tired and faded eyes, Father Oculist felt slivers of glass in his conscience. He had sinned against charity and against obedience. He had spoken rudely and so angrily to this man who towered above him in so many ways. And perhaps he had sinned also against humility. Was it or wasn't it true that he had labored so long and so zealously over that damned reading glass, not for love of Father Pat, but in the hope that the great man might publicly praise his work?

" 'My hand's all right,' he said stubbornly. 'Sometimes it's good to bleed. Blood redeems.' He thought that by suffering a little pain and losing a little blood he could, partly at least, atone for his sins.

" 'You are harder than the diamonds I brought you," he added with an irony of his own which he didn't know he owned, 'as a token of the admiration, love, and esteem of everyone in the university.'

" 'Also harder than the reading glass you forgot to mention,' Father Pat said. 'Sit down and let Father Surgeon look at that hand.'

"Father Pat stood for an unendurably long time staring at all the things he held in his hands. And he began to weep!

"Nearly everybody in the audience rose as if to see better, as ring fans do when the champion has been hit with a right to the jaw and is about to fall.

" 'And tears redeem,' Father Oculist said directly into the mike. 'God loves tears. He demands tears! He rewards tears!'

"Father Pat, obviously irritated, turned to him asking:

'Now who made a preacher out of you? Didn't I tell you to sit down and hold hands with the doctor? Well do it! And keep quiet!'

"He turned again to the great mass of people he could barely see. He was still letting the tears roll down his cheeks. But he was smiling now; and there was a shine in his eyes astonishing to behold.

" 'It was only the mercy of God that kept me from sending Father Dave as a missionary twenty years or so ago to the God-hungry and God-ignorant inhabitants of Westchester and the Bronx. Within a year he would have poisoned all of them with his innocent heresies. And all South Heresy would be ready for contamination. Blood and tears! These are his only antidote for crime and corruption, it seems. "Bleed and weep and you will be saved! Horse feathers!'

" 'Shame,' a woman in the balcony cried. 'You're blaming him for what happened. You're taking your spite out on him! Shame on you, Monsignor! And you know very well that blood and tears do redeem!'

" 'Ah,' the Monsignor remarked, 'there never was a hen that didn't cackle when she laid an egg. There never was a chick that didn't think her egg was new, fresh, perfect— even though it had been lying for weeks in her hidden nest. Sometimes you have to throw an egg hard against a rock— say the rock of Peter—to make the hen smell her error. And sometimes the poor bird sits on a china door knob some joker thrust under her. Then her cackle is louder and prouder than ever.

" 'Dear lady, blood and tears most certainly do not redeem. Only love redeems. Perfect love. And surely it isn't news either to you or to Father David that we have already been redeemed? Haven't you even heard of Christ's Emancipation Proclamation? It's been in existence for more than 1900 years. It was written in glorious red letters.

" 'Blood and tears! We forget God's part in our redemption. We forget we are already redeemed. We were redeemed by love. And we owe God love. If we repay him with our love, he will give us tears of contrition to wash us clean. If we love him very much, he may even give us the crimson joy of holy martyrdom! But our blood and tears? Again—horse feathers! Why do we always forget God's part in our redemption? Because we want all the credit!' "

CHAPTER 8

THE MODERN DELITHERIUM

The words filtered through my sleazy mind as I sat lazily on the hilltop and looked at sun and sand and sage and cactus barbs and graves and ruins. The words concerned a primitive man (whose name it seems was Smith). "A man sat on a rock and sucked his thumb; a delitherium wandered by and scared him some."

The village that lay in shards and shambles all around my rock was ancient enough to have known all the prehistoric monsters we meet only in print today. "It is at least six thousand years old," Poldy kept repeating, "maybe more. And thousands of Indians lived here."

Poldy (a pet name for Leopold) was born in this part of Arizona and often visited this place when he was a boy. He had invited me, Clarence O'Neill, and one of my nurses, "Mitzi Mitzi," (a special pet name for Ray Gene Neubig) to return to it and hunt for arrowheads and pieces of pottery. We had driven there in Clarence's little yellow bug from the oasis of the Casa.

Poldy is three or four years older than I am and I am ankle deep in the eighties, but he climbed the steep side of that hill without even breathing hard. I had to stop and rest several times. Clarence and the nurse stayed with me, "ready to catch me if I stumbled." (There was once a time not too many years ago when friends used to say things like, "Don't you think you should let somebody else drive the car? Suppose you dropped dead at the wheel. A brand new car!" Or, "Don't lock that door from the inside. Suppose something happens. How are we gonna get the body out?")

I made the top by myself taking it easy. I looked around and chose my rock—the softest available. I sat a long time, thanking God for the beauty and the peace I saw and felt and for the ghosts of eternity that haunted the place even in the glorious sunshine.

"Six thousand years ago," Poldy said, "and now nothing but graves." He and Clarence looked for arrowheads. Mitzi Mitzi took up a collection of pottery scraps. I just sat on my rock content to realize that no delitheriums were likely to bother me and tried to bring the ancient village back to life.

The young men would be in the adjacent hills hunting game. The older men and the cripples would be chipping pieces of flint, each striving to make a more perfect product than anybody else.

Some of the women would be farming the little patches of maize way down there at the foot of the hill. The others would be making pottery, grinding corn or getting food ready for the hungry hunters. Some, of course, would be nursing their babies and trying to hush the screaming demons running all over the hilltop and threatening every minute to trip and go rolling down into the never-never land.

And, of course, there would be someone always at the fire ready to send up smoke signals at the approach of any stranger.

A constant watch was kept. A man could see strangers coming from any direction. And naturally, every stranger was an enemy with envy and larceny in his heart and a wicked knife in each of his treacherous hands.

The children had the sharpest eyes and they were trained

to be alert. They were trained to fear and to hate, to distrust and to kill.

I wondered what had killed these people. Was it one of those fabulous dragons? Was it plague? Was it an invading army that had come up the sides of the hill at night?

"Hate massacred them," a voice said. "Hate that grew among them. Hate that grew with the hours. Implacable hate. Family hate. The worst kind of hate."

Maybe I heard the words. Maybe I just made them up. I was somewhat disturbed at the time for one of my magic desert windows had opened and I was looking at the re-run of a drama I had seen enacted.

I was standing in another hilltop village, a village far away, village beyond many great waters, a village that may be as ancient as the graveyards in Arizona, yet is still alive and growing.

At that time it was rocking with an unusual joy. The narrow streets were filled with people dressed in their best. Two hundred or more men were dancing in the street, arms locked in a chain that extended for a great distance down this street around the corner and up another street. Their feet were dancing in a fascinating rhythm. Their bodies were swaying in harmony with their feet. And they were singing about the beauty and the rapture and the sheer wonder of young love.

The women were everywhere but they were subdued. They were even more excited and happier than the men by the looks on their faces. But they had work to do. They had to hurry to the banquet place and get everything ready.

A young man and a young woman had been solemnly married that morning in the church and everybody in the village had come to rejoice with them; to shower gifts upon them and to pray for their happiness.

Here in this dead and buried village in Arizona I watched the wedding procession so many thousands of miles away and felt the exultation I had felt when I first saw it. And then once more I saw the old priest standing in the blistering bright sun, holding an umbrella over him, sobbing and weeping like a child who had lost his mother. He was a tall, strong, great-shouldered man with white hair and an extraordinary long white beard.

"Joy pulses through the flock like blood through the heart," I remarked to someone standing near me. "And the shepherd looks on and weeps as though this were a funeral and not a bridal ceremony."

"In due time," my companion explained, "the two people so full of love and happiness today will give birth to children. And in due time these children will grow up to turn against them. The people see only the romance. The priest sees the tragedy to come."

On a day just like this some years before, a pleasant and most friendly stranger had come to the village and let it be known that he loved the people and yearned to do something wonderful for them. He was rich. Why shouldn't he build a school for the children? He had looked everywhere in the village but nowhere did he find a school. He had learned, he said, that the priest was the only teacher. Alas, the priest was getting closer and closer to his reward. What would happen to the children when the good old man was gone?

The people were delighted to think their children could actually go to a school as children did in other villages. And the priest was delighted too— for a little time.

The school was built. There was a day of jubilation, a day of thanksgiving and hope and civic pride. It was a free school. Even the books were free. One thing only was required. The students must be baptized.

The priest and some of the elders of the village protested that every last one had not only been baptized but confirmed as well. They had been baptized into a faith taught by one of the twelve Apostles and need not be baptized again.

But the man who ran the school explained patiently, politely and repeatedly that another baptism was required, was absolutely imperative. No baptism, no free education.

The priest fell on his knees and prayed fervently when he learned his flock would not listen to him. What difference did another baptism make, they demanded, so long as their children stayed in school?

To show his appreciation of their attitude the school master provided many treats for the children. He even went to the expense of buying a beautiful and somewhat frightening big red bus in which to take them out into the countryside for picnics.

No child in the village had ever seen so marvelous a creation. Certainly none had ever dreamed he would be permitted to ride in such luxury and such glory. No one had even dreamed of going out of the village on any sort of journey.

The children going to school were the envy of all those too young or too old for school. And they were the pride and joy of their parents. They were listened to with awe and great respect. They were, everybody said, the hope of the country, the hope of the whole world. They were allowed liberties not given other children. Frequently they were excused from going to church—because they had to study or because the school master had his own religious services for them—and his own little gala parties.

Gradually the time arrived when the children refused to go to the church when they said that ikons and statues were heathen idols. Some even spat on the picture of Our Lady! A slow leak of gas. A sudden explosion.

The little community that had held so much love and happiness and simple faith was slowly but surely turning into a place of anger and tears and threats and fear and bitter hate.

A year or so after the joyful wedding day the priest gave up his life for his flock. And the young bishop who wept with him on his deathbed and sang Alleluias for him in his funeral mass ordained a young man of the village as the new parish priest.

He invited the school master and his helpers—he had several by this time—to attend the ordination services and to be his special guest at the banquet. When all the guests had eaten the bishop rose to speak:

"I have ordained this young man because he is worthy," he said, "and because he is capable of tending this flock. But I am not going to appoint him at this time to this or any other parish. I am instead going to make a proposition to you teachers. I make it sincerely and honestly out of the very heart of my heart.

"I will send this priest elsewhere and give to you all I have in this village, this holy parish. I will give you the church and all the property and all the people too, if you will teach the children to love and not to hate!"

The teachers could hardly wait to get out of the banquet place. Then they hurried to their superior in a distant city and told him breathlessly about the mad bishop and his mad challenge.

Late that night after a long and tedious journey the superior hammered on the bishop's door and demanded to know what trick he was trying to play. The bishop welcomed him, gave him something refreshing to drink, and repeated what he had said to the teachers.

"Do you actually mean that?" the visitor asked.

"I was never more sincere. I will make the same proposition to you. I will give you every church, every hospital, every orphanage, every old peoples' home and every other building in my diocese—including this one. And I will also give you all my sheep—if you will promise from your heart that you will teach the children to love and not to hate.

"You have, without meaning to of course, taught these little ones to hate the Faith that came down to them from Jesus Christ and his Apostles. You have taught them to hate their native village, their ancient ways, their poverty, their old-fashioned parents. You have taught them to fear and distrust and hate one another. And some day you must realize they will hate you and your people with an almost murderous hate for what you have done to them."

Tears sprang into the visitor's eyes. (I was not there but I know what I write). He wept as the old priest wept for his lost sheep that day of the line of singing and dancing men.

"Bishop," he said, "You remind me of Solomon who threatened to cut a child in half so that he could find the real mother. You, too, would give up your child to insure its happiness and its life. Give me time to decide what I must do."

Maybe the village so very far away will die of hatred.

Maybe it will take on a new life because of the love of an old priest and the wisdom and prayers of a bishop. Who knows?

I tried to open the window that looks on heaven so that I might learn how the story will end. But I could not even coax it to give me so much as a peek. It sticks. It sticks. It sticks.

As I went down the slope from the ruins of the Indian village around sunset I wondered if all civilization today doesn't live on a towering mountain where it can watch its neighbors and prepare in fear and suspicion and hate to greet them with the new home-made flint arrowheads.

We, too, teach our children to hate. What can we expect of them when they are grown?

Hate: the modern delitherium. It wandered by and scared me some. I was glad to get back to my desert cell where all is peace and love and to say mass for peace on earth, good will to men.

CHAPTER 9

TAILOR-MADE CROSSES

Blessed be the desert, the trysting place of man and God, the wasteland that gives and does not take away the strange poustinia on the edge of heaven, the barren soil in which God's choicest vineyards grow. And blessed be the Winslow, Arizona, hospital, the oasis that sheltered me for the forty days and nights of Lent.

There daily the Lord's caravans arrived, bearing graces I cannot name, as I did not unload his camels. All I know is that they mysteriously changed misery and pain into happiness and even great joy! This still amazes me.

The beautiful adventure began just before Lent. A few words I said during the Divine Liturgy put it into action.

"If you intend to carry a cross during Lent," I said, "don't make it yourself. No man can be trusted to fashion a cross for himself. It will be much too light or much too heavy. Get a tailor-made cross. Let God be your tailor. He'll fit you perfectly. He gives his beloved crosses every day, for his purposes, and for your good. Little crosses or big ones. Annoyances. Trials. Disappointments. Rebuffs. Aches or pains.

"He has many such gifts for you and they are all good, whether you like them or not. If you dislike them, accept them anyway—just because they come from God—just because they are a proof of his love—although you may not think so. Accept them. And try to enjoy them!

"God will give you the grace to be happy even with a toothache—if you accept it as his will and if you realize that, in actually suffering for him, you are a highly privileged soul.

"Don't just cut out cigarettes or candy. Cut out your own desires, and listen to the Lord."

A few days later the desert claimed me; and I seemed to hear the voices of many wanderers. Christian and Moslem and Jew with voices lifted in praise to God, thanking him for the long good day, for the water given to the goats and the sheep and the dogs, and for the food the men and animals had eaten. I heard them and wanted to join them, but my throat was sore, and I could neither kneel nor stand up as those nomads did.

And I could hear the voice of a doctor: "Six weeks here and you'll be going home."

Six weeks! Here on this particular bed! I thought of the words St. Teresa of Avila is reported to have said. "Lord, if you treat your friends this way, it's no wonder you have so few of them." I don't believe St. Teresa said anything like that, but I felt for a moment like repeating that rebuke to the Almighty. Then almost immediately I was given the grace to repeat the words of Our Lady, "Be it done unto me according to your word."

God *does* give his friends royal gifts!

My bed was prim, snug, and tight. It didn't look like a cross. It didn't feel like one, but there was something ominous in those beautiful clean sheets. They looked and felt like a shroud. They made me understand that I had been pitched, hand and foot, into a linen cell. I was as trapped as a caterpillar in a silk cocoon. Would I escape only as a butterfly? So be it! God gave me a curious happiness and I went to sleep.

This was on Sunday, February 21, while all the Christian world outside the hospital was getting ready for carnival celebrations.

That strange feeling was within me when I woke. God must love me a lot to give me six weeks of pain and weakness! I who loved him so little! Why didn't I love him madly?

"Well," I argued, "it must be love to accept his will, no matter how it hurts. It if isn't, I am just a poor misguided country boy. This is not only a privilege; it's also a job. I get paid a penny a day like everybody else in his vineyard; and I can spend those pennies from heaven for everything I want. I can help the 'bums,' the alcoholics, the women of the streets, the priests and nuns who have run away from home, the handicapped, the poor, the sick, all those who sin through weakness rather than through malice. Better still, I can give all those pennies to Our Lady and let her have a glorious shopping spree.

"Lady, the money's all yours! Spend it for what you want."

I was so pleased with myself and my nobility—big deal!—that at first I paid no attention to the noise that came from the other half of the room. I had seen my fellow patient, but not clearly, for he was encased in an oxygen tent. I didn't know what was wrong with him. I hadn't particularly cared. He lay in a bed like mine. There was only a sliding curtain between us; but he might as well have been in another desert for all he meant to me.

As the noise continued and grew in pitch and volume, I lost my feeling of holiness and joy. I was annoyed. I was irritated. I was angry. And, of course, I was indignant.

I was sick enough! Did I have to put up with this racket

too? Would it go on all night? Should I ask the nurses to put me in another room? Or should I ask them to take that man away?

My indignation was somewhat abated by my curiosity. What was the fellow doing? What was that sound?

"Every woman in Winslow," I guessed, "has let her bathtub overflow. At the same time, the mayor and the councilmen of the city are driving a huge cylindrical tank of water over the bumpiest streets. The tank is filled with marbles—'aggies, brownies, blueys, and glasseys,' taken from the boys to punish them for neglecting their adorable little sisters."

The frightful racket after a long, long time ended with noises that suggested every housewife had pulled the bathroom plug and the water was going sulkily, reluctantly, rebelliously down the drain, sobbing and strangling on its way.

"You don't like your neighbor?" a silent voice asked me. I answered, with my usual flippancy: "He does not warm the cockles of my heart."

Stupidly I began to wonder about the word "cockles." I knew it meant the most inner parts of the heart. But how come? I thought of the girl who rolled her wheelbarrow through streets wide and narrow, crying "cockles and mussels, alive, alive-o." Likewise, I remembered the rhyme about silver bells and cockle shells and pretty maids all in a row.

Now that the noise had stopped I could, I thought, amuse myself with the vagaries of English words. I was so full of myself I actually forgot the voice had spoken to me.

It spoke again. This time I recognized it. The voice that speaks from behind one of my desert windows (the one that always sticks). It is the voice of an angel? Of Our Lady? Of the Lord himself? I do not know. I do know it is the voice of heaven.

"Someone," it said gently, "has sown cockle in the wheat field of your heart."

The wheat field of my heart! That certainly was the voice of heaven, always hitting where it hurts, always gift-wrapped in poetic phrases.

Cockles: weeds, not shells.

I had forgotten they were weeds.

"An enemy hath done this," I answered automatically.

"Aye, your worst enemy. Yourself. Forgive yourself. Love your enemy. Then forgive your neighbor for disturbing your previous silence. He is merely trying to stay alive.

"What you heard is his humidifier, spraying the oxygen so that it will give his lungs its very best. Why don't you pray for him? He's much sicker than you are. Maybe you were sent here for his sake. Maybe he was put next to you for your sake.

"O.K.," I said. "I'm tough. I can take the noise if I have to. Of course I'll pray for him. I'm a priest. I'm supposed to pray for people, though I forget it often. Thanks for reminding me."

Three or four times I prayed for my neighbor and went back to sleep.

Three or four times that night I heard that horrible humidifier hideously harass the silence and the darkness of the room.

Then, along toward morning, I woke with a start. I was filled with dread, for the room was quiet. Sinister quiet.

I wanted to get out of bed and see what had happened. But I was too weak. My heart, usually as steady as a cock, was suddenly as steady as a loose tooth.

I wanted to ring for a nurse. I couldn't. All I could do was to say to myself, "No, God, no. He isn't dead! He isn't dead!"

Abruptly, without any warning whatsoever, every bathtub in Winslow began to overflow. And that giant tank began to roll again. But this time I thought—in my crazy joy—this time it was filled with broken china—pieces of dolls taken from all the little girls, to punish them for "snitching" on their innocent big brothers.

I said a thousand or more thank-you-Lords and drifted back to sleep.

While I slept the doctor took away the humidifier and gave my friend a simple mask—which made no noise at all.

The doctor sent me to the Casa after forty days. I spent the rest of Lent there in a bed. I rose at Easter and, for the first time in fifty days, put on my clothes and walked outside to look at the sun. And I discovered a tremendous truth.

The rarest Lenten flowers and the loveliest Easter lilies bloom only in the scalding sands of the desert.

CHAPTER 10

WORLD'S GREATEST FOOD BARGAIN

A very pretty girl laid me an egg this morning. She laid it on my plate at the round table in the dining room of my oasis in Winslow, Arizona.

She laid it on a beautiful blonde piece of toast, a flat, thin, squarish toast dressed in butter that looked like satin and with a sort of black fringed mantilla draped with exquisite carelessness over one of its soft shoulders.

The egg was white and shiny and quivering with delight as if it had just stepped out of its luxurious hot bath and unshelled itself. It was resting comfortably on its warm tan couch.

I thanked the Lord that it was there, then thrust the tines of a fork into its heart and opened it wide so that its golden blood and water gushed forth. I sprinkled a little salt into the wound—not real salt of course, but the kind a nurse gives to those who are always supposed to obey commands such as, "if you like it, spit it out."

When I had prepared the egg and the toast for the morning sacrifice I looked around with my groping old eyes and saw a glass of blushing cranberry juice, a steaming cup of tea, and something round, soft, and sort of yellow. It smelled like a grapefruit. And, by golly, at the touch of my spoon it turned itself into a grapefruit!

There were five girls at the table with me. Four staff workers and my nurse. They were eating ordinary buttered toast, grapefruit, and coffee.

Well, that's their usual breakfast. Some days mush and

milk and a little sugar. Sometimes jam or jelly for their toast and sometimes just good old-fashioned country margarine.

To see them more clearly I put on my "cataract" specs. (Author's note: a cataract in this case is not a waterfall; it is not a cascade. It is the beam the doctor takes out of your eye so you can see the gleam in your neighbor's eye. He gives you a special lens to look through that does something terrific to colors. Baby, you never saw color before you got uncataracted! What you see now is the way red, orange, blue, yellow, green or violet makes up for what you didn't see during your first eighty years. Shout for joy to the Lord who created color!)

I looked my fill at the young women and thanked God again. I still maintain that a woman is the greatest proof of God's love for men.

After I had savored these five priceless princesses, his gifts to me, I looked at the color combination of my breakfast. Wow! How good God is! He gives us not only food—and the appetite to appreciate it and the taste that makes it twice blessed—he gift-wraps it with reds and browns and yellows and all the other colors and tints and shades he has made for us. How very, very much he loves us!

At six o'clock (after a few hours of writing) a hot and aromatic mystery was set before me at the round table. My nurse cautioned me not to touch it lest I burn my fingers. I ventured to ask her what gourmet miracle she had prepared for me.

"Call it casserole neubig cheddarton ham," she said. "I put a lot of things into it. I never follow any recipes. I cook with my heart as well as with my mind. The green stuff on the side of the plate is asparagus hollandaise and peas ın

horseradish cream sauce. For dessert you will have pears a
la parish Madre de Dios with a special sauce I whipped
up."

All my meals in this and every other desert cell I have
ever occupied have been prepared by someone who loved
food and knew how to prepare it. *Deo Gratias!*

The back window in my desert swings wide open to show
me my grandmother making bread, kneading dough in a
big enameled blue pan in the kitchen and putting a big
boiled potato into the mixture.

Nobody ever made better bread. Gran was proud of her
bread but she was like my nurse who could never give me a
recipe for it.

Another vision is that of my mother beating flank steak
with a cobbler's hammer. My grandfather, Martin
Doherty, left his tools to my father. They were all he had to
leave. He made a pair of shoes that took first prize in an
exhibition at the Chicago World's Fair in 1892, but that
didn't make him either famous or rich.

Eventually, "Courageous Nell" as we called her, sub-
stituted another tool, one that tore the meat as it pounded
it. Mother would spend hours at this steak beating. Flank
steak was cheap but tough. You had to kill it again to make
it tender. Love is the best hammer of all. She hammered
hell out of that steak with her love.

The window closes and opens and I watch a Mormon
cowboy somewhere in Utah—somewhere near Moab—
trying to laugh and not curse over a batch of sourdough
biscuits he had ruined.

"I wanted them to be so good," he says. "Look at them. I

betcha a horse could break his teeth on any one of them. I betcha I could kill Old Chief Posie with one of them there things if I could throw that far."

Posie was a leader of the Utes (or was it Piutes?) in that part of the state. He had rescued one of his men who had been put into the local pokey by the local sheriff; and he had killed or wounded a deputy or two in making his escape.

This was fifty years ago and some of the details escape me. I remember he had a rifle that was able to shoot with accuracy over a range of three miles. The sheriff formed a posse and set out to capture him. The United States Marshal stationed at Salt Lake City joined the posse the next day. I arrived from Los Angeles a day or so later.

I was the western correspondent of the *Chicago Tribune.* I was supposed to cover "unusual" stories anywhere in the West. This was the last "Indian uprising." I couldn't resist it.

We stayed three miles and a few rods from where Posie was supposed to be, slept in blankets under the stars or in some friendly Mormon house, ate "wild west" food, and hired some of the posse as couriers to ride our news stories to the nearest telegraph office.

I remember only one Indian distinctly. An old Navajo. I remember him for what he said and for the way he said it. "White man give Indian two things. Give him whiskey. Give him hell. Now white man take away whiskey. Indian have only hell." I thought they talked that way only in books. Could he have been quoting?

I shall never forget the cowboy cook.

We sat in silence for some time, I recall, while he threw new mesquite branches and jack pine cuttings on the flames and prepared another batch of biscuits. The stars, the campfires of the angels, seemed to be just a few hundred feet above our heads. It was a magic world, a magic night.

When the biscuits were done the cowboy tossed me one. It almost burned my hands. I baptized it in melted butter and confirmed it in strawberry jam. Mama mia! That was love!

The storm of a great thought slammed that window shut and opened the one that looks on Galilee.

And there was Jesus!

He stood on the pebbled shore of Lake Tiberias in all the splendor of the risen sun, bending over a fire of charcoal. He was baking bread and fish for some of the disciples!

Oddly enough I smelled not burning charcoal but burning mesquite and pine.

The apostles were coming in. They had fished all night and had taken nothing until he had called to them and ordered the net to be cast into the water on the right side of the boat. Lo, it had immediately been filled with big fish, "one hundred and fifty-three in all."

I am sure that if I had looked more closely I would have seen a skin or two of wine in the cool shadow of a rock and also a vessel filled with honeycomb. But I saw only Jesus—divine love preparing food for his beloved!

Whoever cooks in Madonna House, or any of its branches throughout the world, cooks with the love of Jesus in her heart—love for the food her father has provided and love for all who will receive it.

Sometimes the cook in the Casa hasn't much to work with. Only vegetables and fruits, given her perhaps by one of the supermarkets. Usually these are good—after they have been trimmed and washed and de-spotted and de-specked. Some of this bounty is delivered to the neighbors. It is not too stale. What is kept is not too little for our staff.

At other times men come bursting into the Casa with a hundred weight or two of fried chicken—or pails and pails of banquet sandwiches—or bags and bags of potato chips—or a dozen fresh doughnuts—or enough enchiladas and frijoles and tacos and tortillas and tamales to last an ordinary family a week or more.

The girls take it all with love—love of God's generosity—love of his permitting them to do a little fasting and a little abstinence. So what if they don't eat meat every day? So what if they have to live on salads for a week or so? Maybe that's what God wants.

These girls are not living for themselves. They are living for the world around them. They are as poor as their poorest neighbor. Why should they have gourmet cooking every day and a gifted cook who can provide it?

Well, why should I have it? Because I am old and getting older and more feeble every day? Because only certain foods are good for me? Or because Our Lord and Our Lady have gotten into the habit of pampering me?

If I could open the window that looks up their way I would ask them. But the window still sticks. I am utterly powerless to alter the fact. So I ask questions through the window.

All I know and all I need to know is that God loves me and loves to feed me what I like.

You know something? He loves you too. He also loves to feed you what you like—what will make you strong and happy, what will give you LIFE.

God give you all a fervent appetite for himself—the gourmet food divine!

Do you think his al fresco luncheon of fish and bread and honeycomb and wine was the best meal ever served to mortal men on earth? If you do, you're all wrong. That meal was nothing at all to the food he serves to all comers every day at mass.

His own divine and human body, his own divine and human blood!

Served with divine and human love. The price? Oh, say an hour's sleep maybe. A lot to ask of course, if you love to lie late abed—but, at any price, the greatest bargain in the world.

CHAPTER 11

LIMPIA NOS, O BIEN DIOS

"Now what's all this stuff about limp pianos?" this wisecracker asked, lowering his puzzled red face so he could get a closer look at me. "I don't buy it. Limp piano players, yes. O.K., I've seen them. And I've seen them stiff and half stiff. But limp pianos? What gives?"

He was a visitor from some jerk-water town like Pittsburgh or Newark or Los Angeles or New York, and far away from home and mama in his holy caravanseria in my private desert here in Winslow, Arizona.

We try to be kind to visitors here, even the rude and the crude and the naive and those who pick up papers from a desk and glare at the writing through red and hostile and unbelieving eyes.

"Not limp," I said gently. It's 'Leemp.' Two words, 'Leempia nos': Spanish for 'cleanse us.' "

His laughter sounded something like a cement mixer going into action.

"Gotcha," he said, stopping the mixing abruptly. " 'Leempia. Like the one about 'what's a wiener?' You say a wiener is a hot dog. I say 'no, it's a horse.' You say no, it's a hot dog. So I explain. 'It's the horse that comes in first in a Mexican derby.' That's the wiener. But that horse doesn't leemp. So what the devil is a leemp piano?" "The word means 'cleanse us,' " I explained again. "Cleanse us from all stain. Its part of the divine liturgy in Spanish."

"You telling me you say the mass in Spanish?" he demanded, his little eyes aimed like a couple of .22 caliber bullets. "I thought you was a mick like myself."

"Oh, I'm much more than that," I said. (I love to brag about myself sometimes, especially to certain people). "I am an American, Canadian, Greek, Arab, Jewish and Spanish mick."

"Sorry," he said, putting down the paper he had lifted from my desk. "Didn't know you had Greek or Jewish blood in you or any such mixture. If I've said anything wrong. . . ."

"No, no," I assured him. "I'm a Greek Catholic priest. I was ordained in Nazareth which makes me a Nazarene. And I'm saying the mass in Spanish because I love the Spanish-speaking people here."

"Is everybody in Madonna House as crazy as you?" he wondered out loud.

"Even crazier," I said. "The other day, the feast of the Annunciation, many of them begged for the privilege of carrying the cross for a year or two or even for the rest of their lives."

He looked furtively at his wrist watch. "Say," he said. "I just remembered I have a date. Gotta get the—the heck out of here. I feel like a barb wire fence. Gotta get loose and unwind."

So he leempt away and I went back to reading the Spanish liturgy.

A long, long time ago, you see, the beautiful Jewish mother of all the Mexicans in this part of the world came down from heaven wrapped with the brilliance of the sun and dancing to the music of a million angels to greet her humble son, Juan Diego, and to ask him to have a chapel built for her.

The Mexicans were speaking their own language then and Our Lady made love to Juan Diego in that language— the love of the virgin mother for a man with a clean and loving heart.

And in a time not nearly that long ago (it was a little over fifty years), I lived in the city of Tampico, Mexico, with my wife Mildred and my son Jack Jim. I became interested in the story of the Virgin's visit because our baby's name translated into Spanish was Juan Diego.

I loved the musical sound of the language and I learned to speak a few words with the proper accent; like for instance, "leche caliente para nino," which means as every schoolboy knows, "warm milk for the baby."

I was running an American newspaper there and had many contacts with Mexicans in the city and the country. I found them the kindest, the most polite, and the most truly Christian people I had ever met.

Later, decades later, I spent seventeen days at the shrine of Our Lady of Gaudalupe in Mexico City and fell deeply in love with her. When Catherine and I left Chicago to live in Combermere, Ontario, Canada, for—so far as we knew— the rest of our lives, we bought a wooden triptych of the Lady of the sun and the stars and the moon and the angels beneath her feet—the picture that heaven painted on the burlap tilma of Juan Diego—the burlap that is still today as sturdy and serviceable as it was four hundred and some years ago!

We put that picture in our bedroom and we have kept a vigil light burning before it day and night for more than twenty-five years.

So it was natural when I heard that Theresa Marsey intended to build a chapel outside the Casa, Madonna

House, in Winslow, that my heart caught some of the light and some of the music Juan Diego caught on that bleak December day on the hill in Mexico.

And something inside me cried out, "Let's give them in that chapel a mass in their own language!"

They are not Mexicans here any more. They do not speak any native language. They speak "good American" because they are expected to and because they are forced to if they want to make any kind of living. But they love the language their Spanish conquerors bestowed upon them.

I am in my eighty-third year and getting older every other day; and you might say I am half-blind. The eye that was relieved of its cataract seems to get better every day especially when it reads through the special lens; but the other eye gets worse and worse. In a soft light I can read the headlines of newspapers and maybe a few sentences of the stories beneath them. However, with my special glasses saddled over my nose I don't know where I'm going. If I try to pour my own tea my aim is pitiably bad. I pour more tea outside the cup than in it.

So how was I going to learn Spanish?

God in his mercy and his Marsey (Theresa, chief servant of the Casa), gave me a brilliant idea.

"Let Miriam translate the divine liturgy from English into Spanish," I said to Theresa. "Let Maureen put it into big letters. And let Kathy and Ray Gene arrange Spanish music instead of Arabic. We'll say a Spanish mass on the day the angel Gabriel talked to Mary in her native tongue."

So a beautiful new missal was compiled for me. And I am laying odds of eleven to six that there is more love of God and neighbor in it than you will find in any of those tomes of splendor and illumination the fervent and artistic monks of the thirteenth century ever offered to the Lord.

While the girls worked with pens and rulers and a guitar and a gifted soprano voice, the chapel began to take shape outside. One day it seemed to me all the kids in the neighborhood were helping to dig the foundations. Spanish-speaking men were doing most of the digging. Two or three blacks shoveled with them and one great, tall, handsome and majestic Navajo insisted on doing his share.

Surely Our Lady of Guadalupe was pleased that day!

Then the rains came and the snows and the hail and the sleet. "Most unusual," everybody said—as everybody usually does.

And through the worst blizzard that ever blundered its way through Arizona came my brother Bill driving his '59 cadillac from Los Alamitos, Calif.

He had recently been through surgery. He had nothing to do but stay in bed and recover his strength. Naturally he couldn't endure that. He arrived in time for the feast and the Spanish mass.

"I suppose you're offering the sacrifice for the chapel," he said. "Theresa will need everything. Vestments. Sacred vessels. A new tabernacle. And especially, money."

"The mass," I told him, "is for all the boys and girls taking—or making their promises today—asking, even begging for the cross of poverty, chastity, and obedience. It is for them, their intentions, their people, and their people's people. Our bishop Jerome Hastrich is giving Theresa the tabernacle. It was a Mexican treasure chest.

"Our Lady of Guadalupe will provide for all the other needs just as Our Lady of Combermere provided for all the chapels we have built in Canada. People who love Our Lady will send everything the chapel needs."

The feast of the Annunciation was one of the most beautiful we have had in this desert. Staring through the window that looks back on the past I can see that the December day we held the first mass in our chapel in Combermere was even lovelier. It was actually like a day in June.

I wish I could tell you what the weather will be like when the chapel of Our Lady of Guadalupe opens its doors—and its motherly arms—to the neighborhood. But the window overlooking that event sticks—the way wet cement sticks to the shoes of all the little angels who walked across it. (Wasn't there some joke about liking kids in the abstract but not in the concrete?)

I was ready to say the entire mass in Spanish that glorious day. But midway through it, sometime after the gospel and the homily, the Spanish words began to jump like grasshoppers all around both my eyes. I began to snap at them.

Then my voice, my gravel and ashes voice, tried to jerk away from me. What could I do but switch to English?

The English words frolicked around me too. But I knew my way through them. I didn't really have to see.

I whispered and coughed my way to the last blessing.

I wasn't embarrassed. I wasn't dismayed. I didn't feel any sense of failure or futility or frustration. On the contrary, I felt triumphant in an odd sort of way. And I had reason on my side for I had learned that whether the priest speaks English or Spanish or Arabic or French or any other language, he speaks with the tongues of angels; he speaks the words of God.

He is the most privileged of all speakers. Even the most exalted of the angels do not juggle divine words so easily, so naturally (even so carelessly), as he does.

His words compel the all powerful to do his will. His words bind God!

I finished the mass with a deep sense of awe and a new and exciting appreciation of the priesthood. And for the first time since I was ordained, I looked a long time into the golden sea of love and mercy in the golden cup I held in my right hand. And I mentioned names I love! Many names, names of the living and the dead. Names of enemies and friends. Names of people I have never met.

The next day and the day after that I had no trouble saying and singing the entire mass in Spanish. And you know something? The Spanish words speak English back to me!

"Limpia nos de toda mancha y salva nuestras almas, O buen Dios!"

"Cleanse us of all stain, and O Supreme Goodness, save our souls!"

CHAPTER 12

ON SAVING POOR FISH AND GOOD THIEVES

It was Laetare Sunday and I, a happy hermit, had a permit to leave my portable desert—I carry it around with me as a turtle carries its shell—and spend a holiday with the four lettuce-eating staff workers of Madonna House in Winslow, Arizona, and my salt moll, Ray Gene Neubig.

Maybe I should explain some things right here. You've all heard of the gun moll, the girl who carries the weapons for the gang? A salt moll carries the substitute salt for her dietetic patient when he goes away from home—or his desert cell.

The holiday began at the round table in the Casa after mass. But it was an odd sort of holiday. If there were even half an ounce of Anglo-Saxon in me, I might characterize it as a jolly day. And if there were the slightest hint of French in me, I might pronounce it a folly day. However there was a lot of fun in it; and a lot of sun in it; and maybe now and then a bit of a pun in it. So it was not at all a melancholy day.

Theresa Marsey started it.

"Flat and toughey?" she asked. "Or fat and fluffy?"

She was holding a platter for me to look at and guess at.

"A riddle?"

"More like a griddle," she said. "Indian fried bread! A donation! How about this one?"

She chose what she liked best. A "fat and fluffy." She slit a nice little hole in the top for me. "Now you fill it full of honey and eat it."

The honey rested in the lower half of a plastic bottle made to resemble a doll. I turned it upside down, pressed its middle on the spot the manufacturer had in mind for the pressure of my thumb, then dared gravity to do its worst.

"That reminds me," I said, "there are two girls in Jerusalem I must write to."

"I know," Theresa said. "You're spilling honey on your hand."

"My cataracted eyes," I said, thankful I had such a good excuse for my clumsiness. I licked the honey off my fingers, upended the dolly again and this time aimed with more precision.

Of course I was helped by all the women watching me. "A little to the right, Father Eddie. A little to the left now—there—steady—that's right. Steady, steady, Father Eddie."

"You know the girls I must write to?" I asked Theresa.

"Carol Honeybun and her pal Helen Breen," she said. "Sometimes it's easy to read your mind—knowing how one thing reminds you of another, and how susceptible you are to any pun, especially one so obvious. Carol Honeybun!"

Maureen said something about a gold fish with a vanished tail.

Of course I could have asked a silly question that might bring me some glimmer of understanding; but one of my desert windows had blown wide open and I saw an old friend who took my mind far away from any vanished tail.

The "skyscraper burglar," as the newspapers called him, was looking in on me.

He used to travel through the tall office buildings of every big city in the U.S.A., every big city except Chicago, and pick an office or perhaps a suite of offices he would like to inspect. At first he carried a little vial of liquid explosive. He dropped it accidentally one afternoon when he was prowling a high rise apartment in Detroit. There was a tremendous explosion but Jimmy got away safely, scampering madly down eight flights of stairs shouting, "Don't stop me. I'm running for a doctor."

That day taught him a lesson. He never carried any kind of bang-bang after that. He didn't have to. He looked for the combination of the safe. Some careful businessman always wrote it neatly on a bright colored slip of paper and put it in a pigeon hole where even a dumb burglar could find it.

In New York or Miami or Kansas City or Dubuque, for all I know, he found a big ornate cut glass goldfish bowl. It was a lovely thing, he told me, and he wanted it. He couldn't steal it without first emptying it. He arranged a row of paper cups on the side of a desk and poured the fish into them, two or three fish to every cup.

You see, he was a sentimental sort of thief. He couldn't bear the thought of killing those pretty fish. He was sentimental about his wife too. He always took a pair of her shoes with him so he would stumble over them when he got out of bed and feel that she was with him if only for a moment.

A burglar's life, however, is not all roses and sunshine and goldfish. No, no. You'd be surprised.

Jimmy bought some goldfish in Chicago. He would have swiped them, he told me, and carried them out in a canteen. But he didn't want anybody to think of him as "just a shoplifter punk."

The goldfish were bad medicine. Very, very bad. Jimmy confessed he had become "too attached" to them. He liked to sit and watch them. His wife was jealous. And she complained.

He was neglecting his business.

Poor Jimmy! What should he do? If he went traveling again who was going to feed the fish? Who was going to talk to them? Who was going to watch them? He should stay in the city but he mustn't go anywhere in the Loop. Too many cops in the Loop. And every one of them on the lookout for him. He would have to try a neighborhood where no cops knew him.

He tried. He got himself safely into a flat not far from his own and was just beginning to enjoy its peace and luxury when cops came pouring in through the doors and windows.

Some snoopy neighbor had seen him and had had nothing better to do than to phone the nearest police station.

Jimmy died in a sort of goldfish bowl—one fitted with unbreakable steel bars. He died quietly in his sleep on a Good Friday morning fifty years or so ago.

I closed the window softly and opened the one that looks on Calvary. I said a word to the first "good thief" and forgot for a long time all that had been said about a vanished or banished or famished goldfish tail. I was too busy thinking of the man who first opened the vault of heaven. He didn't have to use "soap," or dynamite like Jimmy. He found the right combination. A prisoner dying at his side presented it to him.

Anybody "down on his luck" can always find Jesus and the key to heaven in any crisis, on any cross or in any prison cell.

After breakfast the girls and I went to the old, old volcanic hills a few miles out of Winslow and looked for petrified wood. We wanted only the agatized and opalized stuff. We threw away everything that had no luster.

I held one plain little hunk of "ordinary" stuff in my hands quite a little time before I let it drop. It was, I reflected, as genuine as the other stuff. It was as old as the other stuff. Millions of years old, maybe billions.

Bah! What was a million years to me? I couldn't imagine even a thousand years.

Did God decide the destiny of souls only by their luster?

Well, only he can judge and see that luster. And only he can give that luster to a soul or to a stone. Every stone and every soul should accept with thankfulness and joy all the luster God can give it.

Can a stone be joyful? Can a stone feel gratitude to God? Ask the stone that used to be a heart.

Suddenly I got tired of walking up and down the mountainous lava hills straining my eyes for lustrous stones and thinking thoughts I could not answer.

"What's all this nonsense about a goldfish?" I demanded.

"Oh," Kathy said, throwing a tin can down the hill so the dog could have some fun chasing and retrieving it, "that's the most extraordinary fish in Winslow. I saw it floating belly up one morning in its little bowl. I ran and told Theresa it was dead. Theresa didn't seem to be at all disturbed. 'Put some fresh water in the bowl,' she said. I did. And the fish came back to life. It does that every day.

But now its tail has vanished and . . . . "

"You did say vanished?"

"Almost vanished. I think one of the children bit a piece out of it. Anyway, something happened to the tail that won't let the fish swim right. He swims with his head down. He never seems able to balance himself. So we thought . . . . "

"We thought," said Theresa, "that you might like to go with us to get some seaweed for him. There's a lot of protein in seaweed. It might restore his sense of balance."

"Seaweed," I said. "Seaweed in the Arizona desert?"

Jimmy was right. People really do get attached to a goldfish!

"Come on everybody," Theresa called. "We're going to Clear Creek Canyon for seaweed."

Two girls appeared over the top of a nearby hill and started running. They beat the dog and his tin can to the waiting car and we headed toward the good old seaweed beds in Clear Creek Canyon!

Clear Creek was only a canyon when I saw it last with a ribbon of dust and pebbles in its bottom. On this Laetare Sunday though, it had thirty or forty feet of cold water pouring through it. Some of my lettuce-loving friends knelt on the rocks and thrust their arms down into the water— giving forth little shrieks of pleasure when the water was too cold.

I stayed in the car until the girls came back.

"Where's the seaweed?" I asked.

"The water's too deep," Kathy said. "But we got some algae. There's oxygen in algae. That may help."

I looked at the goldfish before I turned in my hermit permit for the night.

It was almost an entire inch long!

Sometimes it takes so little to make a happy day. (I still had the smell of honey on my hands and the taste of honey in my mind).

CHAPTER 13

FATHER MARTIN OF TOURS

My kid brother Marty once said, "I don't want to be just a signboard, one of those priests who just points the way to heaven but never goes there."

So he's gone to heaven and taken his signboard with him. He died a few days after his seventy-fourth birthday in St. Mark's Hospital in Long Beach, California. He, his brother Tom, and his sisters Kathleen and Eileen, all carrying crutches or canes, had just come back from a two weeks cruise up the Inner Passage to Alaska. Marty decided he and the family needed the relaxation and the pool on deck to heal or solace their many ailments. Shortly after the trip, at our brother Bill Doherty's house in Los Alamitos, California, Marty began spitting up blood. He was rushed to the hospital against his wishes and there he died. And all the windows in my portable desert have been shaking and opening and closing ever since.

The family had called Saint Marty not only its bachelor priest and the black sheep of the family, but also Saint Martin of Tours.

Every year Marty planned a tour for all his brothers and sisters who could go with him. He never quit being a teacher. He wanted people to see God's world and love it as he did. I was with him one day in Portland, Oregon, when he almost wept because people were so ignorant of the beauty all around them.

"Would you believe it," he said, "There are hundreds of girls in this part of the world who come back from England or France or Italy or someplace else abroad and absolutely shriek about the beautiful things they saw, when they could have gone up the Columbia River for instance, or to the Yosemite Valley or even the Grand Canyon. They have never seen those places and they probably never will. Poor dumb-bells! They spend their money for penny candy and never for ice cream."

Marty was the youngest of what we call the "big four" in our family. He was the gentlest of all the eleven children of "Old Butch" Doherty. To my knowledge he never had a fight in his whole life. Also to my knowledge, he never had any particular girl friends. I think he always wanted to be a priest. The time for the fulfillment of this wish came in Chicago nearly fifty years ago when he was a crime reporter like the rest of the "big four." Bishop Edward Howard of Portland, Oregon, was passing through Chicago looking for priests for his diocese. Somehow he and Martin met and the bishop sent Martin to Rome to become a priest for the Oregon diocese. Marty lived in the North American College and later wrote a book about it called *The House on Humility Street.* He wrote this book and gave it to me to peddle. I gave it to a literary agent in New York who lost it. Marty had no duplicate so he wrote it again from memory and sold it himself. It was a very good book. Until that time we, his brothers and sisters who were all somehow connected with newspapers, had read him out of the family. He was not a journalist. He had left us for a trade school. He was the black sheep. When the book was printed we welcomed him back into the fold.

Marty, like most of the Dohertys, loved to talk about himself. But the way he talked anybody would think he had two heads and had left the brighter one home that morning.

". . . So Father Mike came to see me that night to invite me to his great forty hours devotions and his car broke down and he had to stay overnight and that night it rained and it rained and it rained. And I said to him, 'Poor Father Mike. All your plans are ruined. There won't be anybody there to begin with. And all your beautiful decorations will be ruined.' He gave me a look of pity. 'Oh you of little faith,' he said, 'oh you of little faith.' It was still raining hard when we woke in the morning and I suggested that we both stay in bed another hour because it would be no use getting to his church on time since it would be impossible to hold the procession. Again he said, 'Oh you of little faith.' So we got up and started out. And it quit raining as soon as we left my parish and the sun was shining when we came into his. It hadn't rained there at all. And we were in time for all the ceremonies. Oh me of little faith. . . .

"I had almost finished mass way down in the hold of the boat when I happened to look up and saw a man falling into the sea. I thought immediately of giving him absolution or of saying a prayer for him. But all I could think of at the moment was 'Grace After Meals.' Maybe God can give him absolution out of my thanks for the breakfast I hadn't yet eaten. Otherwise the poor fellow is in great trouble. . . . "

The one window of my desert that keeps opening most often and widest is the window that looks on the church of Our Lady of Grace, our old parish church in Chicago where Marty said his first mass.

My folks had invited hundreds of relatives and acquaintances and, of course, friends—everybody they knew—to come and get Father Marty's blessing.

After the mass, Marty blessed all the people at the altar rail. He must have walked a mile or so back and forth. When the church was emptied, except for his parents and three of his brothers, Marty vanished into the sacristy. All this time my father, a police captain, had stood near the open door of the church swollen with happiness and pride ushering everybody down the aisle. "This way, this way, right this way. Father Marty will bless you." A few minutes after Marty had gone into the sacristy, Aunt Taisy came in with a group of people. Aunt Taisy, who had lived next door to us at one time, was limping badly. My father helped her down the aisle. "Father Marty will bless you. Father Marty will be out right away." I was watching him, a trifle wistfully perhaps. How proud he was of his red-headed son. How he loved to repeat that name, "Father Marty." Would he have put that much love and pride into his voice if it was Father Eddie who had just said his first mass? Perhaps he would. But I had not become a priest. Marty had.

Aunt Taisy and her friends remained a long time waiting for Marty. My father walked down the aisle to them. "Father Marty will be right out," he assured them. He walked back toward the door. He started toward the sacristy. He changed his mind. "Marty," he yelled. "Come out here, damn it, and bless these people!"

The window that looks on heaven still sticks but maybe God can hear me through it and maybe Marty can hear me also. So I shout, "Marty, come back here, damn it, and bless all these people who mourn for you and bring back that signboard that points to heaven, damn it! I want it."

CHAPTER 14

PLEASE TOUCH

The old girl finally took her bony hard knee out of my chest and I felt well enough to totter over to my typewriter and get a few things on paper.

When the old girl comes for a visit or a long stay there's nothing for a man to do but lie still, swallow a pill now and then, waltz with Our Lady through a rosary or two, and think of things it would be nice to put on paper—maybe for *Restoration*. Once in a while the patient gets a chance to grab a pad of paper and a pen from a nearby table, desk, chair or over-turned wastepaper basket and scribble some notes before the nurse comes back and takes some notes herself.

Only when Aunt Jina un-knees herself can you get anywhere near your Underwood-Olivetti to record these golden assets.

And that's what I was doing on this day I was going to tell you about. I had written such lines as these when he came in. He, you all know, is Father Briere.

"Birth is God's kiss of welcome to this life. Death is his kiss of welcome to eternal life—and who shall say he kisses the dying penitent less fervently than he kisses the dying saint? I see Almighty God looking down on all us rusty and dusty and dented and dimmed tin soldiers. He looks at us with love and pity, something in the way a human father looks at the toys his little son had loved so very, very much."

Father came in and seemed glad that I was out of bed and busy. "It's a wonderful day," he exclaimed. "Beautiful sunshine. A delightful breeze. Woods full of your favorite mushrooms. How'd you like to get a basket and come with me?"

"I'd have to put shoes on," I objected.

"Well then," he said, "What about the rose quartz mine? You must have heard that Mr. and Mrs. Jerry McCoy have a contract to deliver ten to fifteen thousand tons to China every month. They've invited us to come see the mine and take home some samples."

I knew the mine. It looks like a rose-pink cloud shining in the sunset on top of a nearby mountain. Only it isn't a cloud, it's red acres of glory on a mountain top in Quadeville.

"Hey," I yelled, "somebody find my shoes."

I had been to the mine before, many times. It was and is one of the natural beauties of this part of the world. I was more than glad to go again. Rose quartz is something like petrified wood and something like jade; only, of course, it's entirely different.

It can be cut and polished to make fantastically beautiful things. The McCoys have some pieces on display in their home that even a priest would love to steal, and probably would, if it weren't for the knowledge that his sin would betray him. Nobody can steal such beauty and not want to show the whole world what he stole.

It really was a beautiful day. I found my shoes. We did go to see the McCoy mine. We did bring home some exquisite samples. We did have a peculiarly wonderful and beautiful afternoon.

Only a crazy mind like mine regards the whole adventure

as one with a weed, a weed he had never heard of before, a weed Mrs. McCoy uses for curing poison-ivy sores on friends of hers.

It's called "touch-me-not," Mrs. McCoy said, "because if you give the seed pod even the slightest touch, it disintegrates in your fingers. Now you take the stem and the leaves of this plant and boil them . . . ."

Right away the windows in my "faithful companion" desert began to rattle and shake and open and shut, all except the one that sticks. (That's the one that looks at heaven).

The front window showed me Christ and Mary Magdalen at Calvary on the first Easter day. Christ was trying to ward her away from him saying: "Don't touch me, I have not yet risen to the Father."

It closed with a bang. The back window—which looks over my past—but never overlooks it—showed me my friend, Father Francis Martin, wrathfully explaining that this "touch-me-not" was one of the most unforgivable translations ever made by any Biblical scholar.

"When Christ called Mary by name," Father Francis said, "Mary undoubtedly clasped him about the knees as he must have known she would do. So, when she had sufficiently shown her joy at his resurrection, he explained that now he must go to the Father and she must not hold him back."

Christ had waited hours, delaying the divine joy of being reunited to the Father, just to say good-bye to a penitent sinner! And the thought occurred to me, he had spent thirty-three years or more—awaiting that reunion—just for the sake of the poor little army of tin soldiers he loved so infinitely much!

Father Briere drove on home with all that rose-pink treasure and all that "touch-me-not" weed Mrs. McCoy was gracious enough to pick for him. All the wild flowers I had picked for Catherine, I didn't give her because they were wilted when we got home. And the back window of my portable desert kept showing me an old friend, Jack Rohan. (Rohan's a good name, don't you think? Anyway, it will have to do).

Jack and I were good friends in Chicago. We worked for the same newspaper. He disappeared somewhere after the beginning of the First World War; and I didn't see him again until the beginning of the next world war. Then he was the "public relations officer" at an army camp "somewhere in the U.S.A." I was a war correspondent and it was his job to take care of me. For an hour or two we were just "Jack and Eddie" and there wasn't a war or a harsh word anywhere in the world. Suddenly he said: "I hear you're married again and also that you're back in the church again. Is that true?"

So we talked about Catherine for another hour or two.

"Somehow I envy you going back to the church," Jack said. "Don't think I ever will. A nun keeps haunting me, Eddie. She was the most beautiful thing you ever saw in a habit. I was ten and she must have been eighteen or twenty. I thought she was holier than the Virgin Mary herself and more believable than all the angels in heaven. That is, until my first communion.

"We were all together, the whole class, before the priest came to say the mass and she made a little talk. 'Now,' she said, 'It may be that the holy water will stick to the roof of your mouth. That often happens when you receive communion. But don't, under any circumstances, put your finger in your mouth to dislodge the wafer. You must never touch God with your hands. It would be the most terrible of all sacrileges. God would strike you dead.' Now the priest puts it in your hands!"

"The Sister who taught us," I remembered, "said much the same thing to us. Yes, God would strike us dead."

"Did the wafer stick to the roof of your mouth?" he asked.

"It did. But I didn't use my finger. I started to, then remembered. Did you?"

"Yes, I dislodged it with my finger without thinking of that nun's warning. And God didn't strike me dead! And I began to believe that everything she told me about religion was a lie. When I walked out of that church I walked out of the church. And damn it, I've been bitter about it ever since."

"I know that bitterness," I said to him.

"Yeah, but you made your peace. I don't think I ever shall. You see, I had an experience with a priest in Ireland. I was in the British army then, stationed in Ireland with a battalion of regulars. That was a bad time, Eddie. The Irish hated us and I didn't blame them. Some of the officers and men were criminals recruited from English jails. The people called us the 'Black and Tans;' we were so many dogs to them."

"It happened that one of my men was killed by an Irishman during the first week of our stay. It was a more or less justified killing but I didn't know it at the time and wouldn't have believed it. I found out later that the soldier had been trying to seduce an Irish maiden and her father or her brother or her lover had beaten the man to death.

"Anyway, I wasn't going to have any more trouble in my

command. I moved into the priest's house and held him as a hostage. I posted a notice in the town square that if anything more happened to anybody in my command, I would shoot the priest and make an inquiry later.

"It worked. The priest and I became warm friends. We never talked religion but there were times I would have liked to.

"We were there for many weeks. On the day we left, the priest and I shook hands. 'Would you really have shot me, Jack?' he asked. 'Father,' I said, 'I'm not sure I would have shot you. And I'm not sure I wouldn't have.'

" 'God bless you, Jack,' he said. 'Sure I'm not worried about you any more. Because now you realize you are a shepherd, as I am, and your flock comes first. You would have shot me. You would have been sorry afterwards, but you would have shot me.' "

Major Jack Rohan! Wonder whatever became of him—and of the pretty little nun whose silly talk made life such a desert for him.

Maybe the Lord has already given them the kiss of welcome to everlasting joy. If so, which one do you think he kissed more ardently than the other?

P.S. Dozens of letters have come to me during my Aunt Jina's lengthy stay, some in sympathy for the death of my brother, some congratulating me on the fourth anniversary of my ordination, some asking me to say masses for relatives and friends.

I will try to answer them soon. Also, I would like to send each one of my readers a rose quartz statuette of Our Lady holding the child to you so you can tickle his toes.

If I'm not able to do it, forgive me. Aunt Jina and I send you our love. The old girl ain't so bad, really, once you get to know her and she sure does make a man think!

CHAPTER 15

THE ERBSTEIN STATION

Today, despite the glory of the sunset of these October trees, I keep thinking of the sower who went out to sow; the honest farmer in the gospel who in spite of everything found that someone had sown cockle in his wheat field.

I am not wishing particularly for the return of spring. The world in which I live, this lovely land of Canada, is more beautiful right now than it will be next spring. There may be a chill rain in the spring when the good man goes out to sow his oats or his barley or his wheat or rye or corn. (And he may spread germs as well as grains).

Standing in the chapel of my portable desert a few days ago I talked about the sower and about the seeds he scatters. It is possible I said a word or two about the sowers who spread gossip or gloom or violence or suspicion or distrust. I don't remember that I said anything of the sort; but who remembers everything? I may even have spoken about those who sow hatred instead of love.

All the time I stood and talked—it wasn't very long—I was looking in two directions. I was looking at the congregation in front of me and I was looking out of the corner of my eye, through the back window—no, no, not the one that always sticks, the one that always opens, the one that looks back into my earlier days.

And there was a real sower, always going out to sow—spring, summer, autumn, winter. A sower of words. He was in some ways the best and the worst criminal lawyer who ever practiced, or mispracticed, in Chicago. Charley Erbstein, of course. Who else?

Sixty years have gone out of the window since I first saw this odd little scatter-good. You may not believe me when I say he was riding a six-foot-six policeman out of one of the court rooms in the old Criminal Courts Building on the near North side. But it's true.

I saw him leap up on the cop's broad shoulders, throw his arms around the cop's thick red neck, club the cop's cheeks with his skinny elbows, and kick him wherever he could with his skinny shorty legs.

And all the time he was screaming, screaming loud enough for judge and jury to hear!

His client had come into this place of justice of his own accord. He had not been condemned. He had not yet been fully tried. And no minion of the law was going to treat the boy so savagely, so unjustly, so illegally!

To my surprise the cop immediately let the boy alone.

"Now," I thought, "he's going to tear that lawyer into little pieces."

That shows you how young and unsophisticated I was.

I thought I was looking at a thrilling drama in real life. A little man brave enough to get himself half-killed to save his client from being ungently handled.

"That guy's a hero," I said to a fellow reporter. "That cop is three times his size. Why does he just stand there though?"

My friend grinned. I couldn't see anything funny. And I was all set for what was going to happen when the cop shook Charley off his back.

What happened was amazing, absurd, and utterly unbelievable. That giant of a man apologized to Charley! "Sure I don't know my own strength, Mr. Erbstein," he said contritely. Really contritely. "I didn't mean to be rough, but . . . ."

The small bald-headed lawyer was not appeased. He took the cop's right arm and raised it as high as he could.

"The arm of the law," he shouted. "it could crush the life out of that poor child and never notice it. Next time, Officer, remember that the arm of the law can be gentle too."

"Yes, Mr. Erbstein," the cop said. "Sorry, Mr. Erbstein." He put his hand gently on the boy's shoulder. "Come along, son," he said.

My newspaper pal was still grinning. "What a ham that guy is," he said. "He should go on the stage. The cop ain't bad either. Wonder how many times they rehearsed that act? Betcha that kid goes free. The gentle hand of the law! Wonderful!" I didn't believe what I had just heard. Such things simply did not happen. That wasn't real! All that lion-hearted courage, all that devotion to the boy, all that beauty about the gentle arm of the law? It was just an act. But why?

"Don't be too stupid," my teacher said. "The kid's being tried for murder. All the evidence is against him. Charley hasn't a chance to spring him unless he can make the jury believe the prosecution is a cruel and clumsy cop with an arm big enough and ruthless enough to strangle the life out of a poor little boy who never had a chance, who was always being pushed around by cops."

Charley was sowing seeds of mercy in the jurors' minds. Charley sowed a lot of cockle in his time but always in the carefully tilled and cultivated fields of the prosecution. He kept his seeds of love and understanding and compassion— and doubt—to sow in the cockles of jurors' hearts.

One nice thing about Charley was that he never tried to fool the press. He was more than frank with most of us. To me he once said, "I don't know much about the law but I know a lot about jurors. If I need a lawyer in the case I can always hire one. But usually I can play the hand alone."

He had one peculiarity in trying a case. He usually made his final plea to the jury immediately after they had returned from lunch. He wanted them in a good mood. He knew that a well-attended belly tends to tenderize and fertilize even the flintiest of hearts. And he needed hearts much more than knowledge of the law. The more pounds of food they ate at the state's expense, the more easily Charley could pound their emotions.

He demonstrated the truth of this on one bleak, cold December day when he was defending a young cabaret singer charged with killing her lover. He made his entrance a few minutes late. He began apologizing to His Honor.

"I'm sorry. It's inexcusable, Your Honor. But as I was passing by the alley I saw a bird cage. Evidently it had been thrown out of a window from that theatrical boarding house just back of the courthouse. There was a bird in it and I . . . . " At that moment he clumsily let the bird, a beautiful canary, fly out of his coat pocket.

"Again I beg Your Honor's pardon and indulgence," Charley said, watching the bird fly all around the court-room taking up everybody's attention.

The judge banged his gavel for silence but nobody seemed to hear him. The bailiff shouted for order but everybody was looking at the bird and everybody was talking and laughing. It was a "good show."

The windows in all the criminal courtrooms were very high and the attendants used a long pole with some kind of gadget on one end to lower the top window or push it up as occasion required. An attendant with one of those poles was now stalking the bird. His face was murderous.

"Don't kill it!" Charley cried out to him. "For God's sake, don't kill it!"

That silenced the court and focused attention on the brute with the pole. That young man, possibly handsomely paid by Charley, finally got the lovely golden singer into a corner of the top window and crushed it to death.

"Got her!" he said, vastly pleased with his skill.

Every juror in the box seemed to shudder as the bird fell, a long golden yellow fall from the top of that high window.

"I'm sorry," Charley said, addressing the jurors. "That poor pretty harmless little bird! Murdered by the long steel-tipped hand of the law! Why? Tell me why?

"I brought it here for warmth, for free air, for its life. Look at it laying there on the floor. It will never sing again, not for you nor me nor for anybody else!"

He turned toward his client and he screamed as though he were suffering both pain and terror. "Here we have another little song bird, gentlemen of the jury. Another creature thrown out into the alley to die. Are you hoping to crush the life out of her too?"

Charley thought he'd get the girl only a few years in the penitentiary. The jury found her not guilty. Probably you would have found the same verdict under the same circumstances.

There are too many stories to tell about Erbstein. But one more must be told here. And that's the one about Father Green.

Charley was indicted on a charge of attempting to bribe a hostile witness in one of his cases. The state's witnesses, half a dozen or more, swore they had seen Charley pay money to a certain man, the star prosecution witness. The witness evidently "disappeared."

Charley cross-examined everybody who appeared against him. Some admitted they disliked him. One or two said they had secreted themselves in an advantageous place before Charley appeared. They suspected Charley was going to bribe their friend and were waiting to catch him in the act.

In his defense Charley called only one witness, a priest who was building a new church on the far south side of Chicago. The question and answers went something like this:

Q. Now Father, you are a validly ordained Roman Catholic priest?

A. Yes sir.

Q. You were recently appointed pastor of your church?

A. That's right, sir.

Q. And the church is not quite finished?

A. Yes, that's right. We still need the Stations of the Cross.

Q. Now Father, where were you on the night of May 16th at half past eight in the evening?

A. In my rectory which adjoins the church.

Q. You were alone, Father?

A. No. We were walking together, you and I.

Q. You're sure of that, Father? It was the night of May 16th?

A. Yes, May 16th and at 8:30. You may remember I called your attention to the clock. I had a meeting of the Altar & Rosary Society at 8:45 and I didn't want to be late.

Q. Then, Father, it would have been impossible for me to

have been standing at Milwaukee and Grand Avenue, and Halsted Street, twenty miles away, like an idiot, with a thousand dollars in my hand waiting for six eye-witnesses to see me bribe a witness who had perjured himself before?

A. You could not have been in two places at the same time, Mr. Erbstein. You were with me. You said your wife is a Catholic and you both wanted to donate one of the Stations of the Cross.

Q. Thank you Father. Now will you explain to the gentlemen of the jury what you mean by Stations of the Cross?

Of course the case was thrown out of court and unhappy things happened to all the people who had testified against Charley.

Maybe Father Green sowed a good word or two in Charley's heart and maybe it was Charley's wife who sowed the seed. Anyhow, something happened to him. He stopped being a "trickster."

He got more joy out of life. He began to laugh at himself. He was fond of talking about Father Green and his church and of repeating; "Today if you go there, you'll find my name on one of the walls. 'Jesus stripped of his garments— by Charles E. Erbstein.' "

Whoever sowed the good word in Charley's heart sowed it in good soil. He was baptized, I learned from old friends, a little while before he died. He died a Catholic.

And looking at my front window I feel like saying: "Charles E. Erbstein, stripped of all his sins by Jesus Christ. Thank you God!"

CHAPTER 16

BEWARE THE DIVINE PICKPOCKET

My most dear relatives, friends and readers, and my most dear fellow staff workers of Madonna House, I send you this year both a merry and a scary Christmas.

I hope it reaches you safely and puts cheer in your heart and a holy fear in your mind.

When and if I have finished it, I will throw it out of one of the magic windows of this collapsible and unelapsible desert. One of my camel-riders will surely find it and immediately go in happy search for you.

I do this instead of sitting down somewhere and writing each and every one of you. My dear Aunt Jina Pectoris has been entertaining me and herself with the pressure of her bony knee. The pressure is right against my poor helpless heart. Poor helpless heart!

Poor Father Eddie? Ah poor Father Eddie!

He lies in bed and rings a bell, and when the bell is rung,
He lies there snug and warm until his breakfast has been brung,
He lies there for his dinner and his after-dinner tea;
And for his supper and his "midnight snack," whatever it may be.
And in between these feeding times, he fasts and takes his pills,
And meekly, oh how meekly, obeys his nurses' wills.

Poor Father Eddie! No priest fasts as often in the day and night as he does. But remember he fasts for you! Incidentally, of course, he prays for you also. And every once in a while he manages to get himself into the chapel to say a mass for you. He does everything but write letters.

Don't blame it on poor Aunty Jina. Blame it on the pills the nurses give him. They make him doze or nap or sleep a little or drop into a profound and lovely slumber.

Poor Father Eddie indeed! The girls who serve him are beautiful and young and strong. They not only bring up his meals, they read his mail to him. He can read the missal with his special lenses but he can't see hand-written or typewritten missives in which the letters are not black and clear.

Some girls take dictation from him but only now and then. He gets tired talking or he goes to sleep. Now and then he signs his name on the back of a check or a money order.

God bless you all especially you whom I have not yet thanked for your donations, your mass stipends, your cards—your sympathy for me in the death of my brother, Father Marty, your congratulations to Catherine and me on our thirtieth wedding anniversary, and for your good wishes on my eighty-third birthday!

When I get out of bed and feel good enough to sit again for a few hours before a typewriter, I'll take over a job Mohammad would have liked. Mohammad, you remember, wanted the mountain to come to him. It wouldn't, so Mohammad went to the mountain. Crazily enough, a mountain of mail has come to me and someday soon, I hope, I will go to that mountain.

Please don't get the idea I am suffering heroically day and night for you and yours. I've got more than a half dozen kinds of pills for relief and I've got a lovely bottle of scotch! (Or I had a bottle). Aunt Jina fools around with the arteries and veins that pump blood through the heart. Whiskey, or alcohol of any kind, goes through the bloodstream and keeps all channels open. If there are any kinks, such as you might swear at in a garden hose, the liquor goes through like an express train, unkinking all kinks, keeping all shipping lanes open. Think of Johnny Walker walking through my heart!

"But," the doctor warned me, "don't drink anything stronger than scotch." My head nurse, Catherine, interpreted that remark. "It means no more coffee for you." Poor Father Eddie! Only tea, water well iced, cranberry juice, ginger ale, lemonade, orange juice, prune juice, and scotch!

So—now that scotch has become medicine I drink it only when I have to! It has lost so much in its translation from a social drink into a mere prescription. And I have to drink it all alone. "Well," I say, "here's to my good health. And here's to yours! And yours! And yours!"

In spite of all this, Madonna House is one of the happiest places in the whole world. Aunt Jina has her pleasant moments—such as a visit from the boys or girls.

One of the girls told me something really lovely yesterday.

"When I first came here," she said, "I wondered about all the laughing I heard. There was one priest who especially puzzled me. Why did he laugh so much? What was he laughing about? Whom was he laughing about? Why did he seem always to be laughing?

"Then one day someone said something beautiful and kind to me and I was so overwhelmed with delight I didn't know what to do. So I laughed. Then I knew why that priest laughed."

Don't worry about me and Aunt Jina. God is here too. And his favorite daughter, his mother, and his spouse. All is well. I may or may not be here for Christmas but I hope everyone of you will be present—in spirit anyway—on Christmas eve and Christmas morning.

You will see an image of the child tucked into a crib beneath the altar. You will love that, of course. But don't look at it too long. It might make you wish that all the world could feel the peace and love of Christ. That may be dangerous. You might decide to do something about it. And people will make fun of you. They may even punish you. Mom may say, "Oh Madge is just going through that religious stage; she'll get over it. Remember when she had the measles? She got over that, didn't she?"

If you are a young man, you may acquire the reputation of a conscientious objector, a pussyfoot pacifist. If we have another draft you may be called a draft dodger or a deserter. And you may be jailed as many times as Dorothy Day. Maybe you should play it safe; look with just one eye.

If you look higher at the right time you will see the priest lifting the body of Christ high above his head.

This is indeed a beautiful, solemn, holy, and awesome sight. It can make your heart stand still. It can make your entire body want to sing. But be cautious. This body of Christ, now so round and white and shiny—and innocent and weak—has been known to batter down castles and to enter millions and millions of private homes—by storm or stealth—and kidnap the bravest and the fairest victims found therein. Some, it is well known, have never seen their homes again; many have suffered unutterable cruelties. Some have died in their prison cells. Few have ever escaped.

If you want him to see the adoration in your eyes, okay, let him see it. But never say you haven't been warned. It may be *you* he kidnaps next. Suppose he whispers, "Follow Me!" What will you do?

If you lift your eyes higher—after a while—you may see a crucifix with that body nailed securely to it. Take it easy now. Just a casual look. Maybe just a peep. That man on the middle cross is the chief thief of the three.

While you are sorrowing over the helplessness of those hands that once commanded the wind and the waves with gestures and that brought Lazarus alive out of his stinking tomb with the beckoning of his finger, that divine pick-pocket is frisking the pockets of your heart and mind and taking for his own everything that is good.

And those feet that are nailed to the cross—those feet that walked on the waters of the sea of Galilee and on the blood of the road that led to Calvary—those feet will kick hell out of your conscience and spur you—perhaps—to the nearest monastic refuge.

At the same time those eyes that seem to hold such awful agony will be looking with all the joy of Christmas into your eyes and deep into your soul.

A merry and scary Christmas. Forgive me for not answering your letters and thanking you for all your goodness.

Besides the blessings of the three Christmas masses I will say for you, I send you the laughter and the joy of Madonna House, the laughter and the joy of God.

CHAPTER 17

THROWING PAIN ON THE FIRE

This particular, personal, portable and most erratic desert stretches today through a small section of Chicago. In a few hours' camel ride from the busy caravanserie which the natives call "union depot," we leave for that curious terminal in a few days to engage an iron camel and follow the Amtrak west.

This iron camel is not really a camel. It is more like an iron dragon, draggin' a serpentine line of waggin' iron wagons across the earth. We go in like Jonah into the whale, only differently, and will be spewed out at our Nineveh which is Winslow, Arizona. The sun shines brightly there and a man can get away from his Aunt Jina for a time and go hunt petrified wood—God's own jewelry—and say mass every day in a brand new chapel.

Say a prayer for my Aunt Jina Pectoris. She's tougher on me than my spiritual director is but much more tolerant than my angelic inspector is. My Aunt Jina sends me here every winter so I may renew my youth like the eagle. The weather is unusual for Chicago. The temperature is in the sixties and the sky, from what I can see of it from my electric blanket tent, is serene and blue. A great contrast to the skies we saw in Canada as we traveled from the house in Combermere to the airport in Toronto. When I say "we," I am not using the editorial "we." I am usually sent places in the custody of a nurse and a priest. One in case I drop dead suddenly. The other in case I don't. We went in a ford. Madonna House is poor but it can afford a ford. That's the insidious thing about listening to too many TV commercials. They not only interrupt the story, they also fill one's head with weird ideas and wants and words.

For instance, take the story of dear old Dr. Kindly. We first see him tickling the throat of his pet viper with an old-fashioned, ink-stained pen-wiper trying to get enough venom for his new cough-drop idea. The phone distracts him. He reaches for it; the viper reaches for his wrist, and clings to it. Immediately two people (husband and wife) come in and begin mopping up the floor, one with a mop and the other with a brush.

Before the floor is finished, a woman enters with a backache, always a nagging backache. She is scarcely out of the way when a man strolls in holding his upset stomach so that you can see all the lovely gas bubbles bubbling. Then a girl is lying on a Florida beach modeling her latest erin go bragh. Thank heavens we go back to dear old Dr. Kindly. He has been called to give a poor boy a new heart. He puts down the phone, drops the viper from his wrist. The viper writhes in agony. The doctor squeezes a few drops of his blood on it and it dies. And of course, in come the dancing girls and boys with their cases of beer. The cameramen disappear discreetly while all is joy and peace. You never can tell how a beer bust will wind up. A good-looking old man shows how, with the proper hair dye, you can bring back those beautiful bronco-busting days and make everybody think you are not yet ninety. Again we see Dr. Kindly. Now he is demonstrating his technique of heart surgery to a group of bored interns. He takes a sharp scalpel and handling it like a piece of chalk makes a diagram on the polished mahogany table. Before we know what he is doing he is holding up a solid mahogany heart and the heart is bleeding. Now it is time to show the new cars, the new snowmobiles, several varieties of soaps and deodorizers. You can squirt yourself dry and walk out into the open air giving everyone the smell of dew-wet pansies. Dr. Kindly's heart bleeds because he accidentally cut off two fingers. But do not grieve. The wise old man pours some venom into a glass of old bootleg whiskey, cleans the fingers, and puts them back on with some of his own peculiar chewing gum. Naturally, they named a scotch whiskey for the doctor and the new TV slogan is "Drink Doctor Kindly's—two fingers will put a new heart in you!"

Why all this nonsense? Maybe my antenna is more disastrous to me than my Aunt Jina. We were riding to Toronto. I was looking at the sky. The clouds had evidently had a vicious fight and the lower skies were filled with black and blue and purple victims who were going somewhere to weep their lives away. I thought of Catherine's words about pain. "When you feel pain, especially the pain of separation, shovel it up and throw it on the fire." You probably don't understand that. It is too profound and needs some explanation. It is absolutely uncommercial.

Now, when a man wants to jump from the ridiculous into the sublime he goes back a few paces and gets a running start before he leaps. So I go back to the morning of my eighty-third birthday in Madonna House. It was early when I woke but there were people in my room. Lots of people. I thought for a moment I was back in the hospital but then I sat up, put on the light, and there were girls all around the screen that protects my eyes from the glaring hall light outside my room. There was another gang in the hallway, boys and girls, and they began to sing, "God grant you many years."

The screen had been redecorated and was covered with paper and painted to represent a tall tree standing by a river. One girl was folding a white paper. She made twenty, thirty or forty folds. It turned out to be a swan. She put the swan on the river. It stuck there. It looked real. She folded several other smaller swans; she folded a lot of people; she folded a bird or two. Another girl was arranging birds to swing around the tree and around the sky above it. A girl was painting a rainbow among the distant hills, and another was putting a beautiful sunrise where it would shine on the rainbow. I was unable to get out of bed that day or the next or the next. But the birthday parties with songs and skits went on for a week or so.

One day someone mentioned Catherine's editorial about prophecy and the burning bush; and from then on, the tree beside the river became to me a burning bush. The front window in my special desert opened wide. At first I thought I had acquired a stained glass window, then I saw it was the burning bush that Moses found on the mountain. It burned brightly and beautifully but did not consume. Some of the flames danced; some were still. Some were blue; some were gold; some were white; some were rose or red or pink. But every leaf and every limb and every twig was burning in peace and harmony and in the love of God and man. I heard a voice outside the window saying, "The first burning bush made by God was the sun. It has been burning for billions of years but does not consume except when little boys let its rays shine through pieces of glass into piles of paper or wood. Scientists tell us it burns gases but they do not say where the gases come from or how they are generated nor why they are not consumed. Madonna House is a burning bush. Every woman, man, and priest in the organization is a flame of some kind. Great or small. Burning with a love that does not consume but gladdens everyone who sees. And the voice of God is present. "Take off your shoes, the place whereon you stand is holy."

The night before we left there was another birthday celebration and I was so moved that I sat by a microphone after dinner and spoke about the burning bush. How Christ came to scatter fire on the earth and Madonna House tries to scatter fire on the earth, the fire of the burning bush. "When you have pain," Catherine said simply, "especially the pain of separation, shovel it up and throw it on the fire. It will go up to the Lord in clouds of incense and the earth will smell sweet and holy for miles and miles around."

So here we are in Chicago awaiting to go west with nothing to do but look at football games and listen to soap sellers, wig sellers, beer sellers, and all the other commercials that dog our TV. This is not only boring but painful. So we throw our pain on the burning bush for the good of all TV commercials, hoping they will all some day find a burning bush of their own.

CHAPTER 18

THE DREAM OF LONGINUS

Maybe it was only a dream. I don't think it was. I think it was a play staged and enacted for me by the angels who accompanied the holy family on their flight into Egypt. But I could be wrong.

Today is January 9, 1974. That may have something to do with it. On January 9, 1904, when I was thirteen years old, I went to the Servite Monastery in Wisconsin to become a servant of Our Lady of Sorrows. In due time I wore her tunic and her rosary but I never did become a monk.

Recently my brother Marty had been adopted into the Servite Order in Portland, Oregon, and given the habit and the rosary. When he died, the rosary came to me. It is a long seven dolor chain with big round beads; and I was saying it last night before I began to dream or to listen and look in wonder.

It was like sitting at my desert window—not of course the one that sticks—the one that looks on Judea and Galilee and all the places ever blessed by the feet of Christ.

Suddenly I was in a little tent somewhere in the desert. It was light there and cool. And there was a heavenly smell.

I saw Joseph come in with his hands full of what I thought were sleigh bells. He was tall. He had to stoop as he came in through the doorway. He was young. He was dark but there were red hairs in his black beard. His eyes were grey and they hurt me. I didn't know why. I didn't know what he was doing with the bells.

"He is dead?" a woman asked.

Mary! She was sitting close to me holding the child!

"Dead," Joseph answered. "Now I'll have to carry you and the baby to Egypt all by myself."

"And the tent?" Mary asked. "And the food? And the water? And the clothing? And the bells? And all your tools?"

"With the help of the angels," Joseph answered, "I can manage the tent and the supplies. We can leave the tools here, and the bells."

He threw the bells on a carpet, making astonishingly sweet music, brushed his hands and smiled. That smile made his face beautiful.

"I don't know why the Almighty should have entrusted you and the child to me and then have killed the donkey! Right here in the bellybutton of nowhere! But he has a reason. Why should I worry?"

"The angels will help us," Mary assured him.

"Yes," Joseph said, "but why shouldn't we help them? It would be nice to carry you, now and then, when you are too tired to walk. Carrying him is wonderful, too."

"Thanks for the 'too,' " Mary said. "The angels are already on the way. Here comes one with a lance in his right hand. Archangel Michael's boy."

She was nursing the child and adoring him. How could she see anyone approaching?

Joseph went to the doorway, opened a flap, and greeted a Roman soldier.

"Your angel," he said, speaking in Aramaic, "has a lance in his right hand and a limping camel in his left."

"Which proves he is an angel," Mary said. "Ask him in."

"It is actually cool here," the soldier said. "And there is fresh air! You Egyptians, you gypsies as we call you, know how to live."

He wiped his brow with a sweaty left hand, breathed deeply, and placed his lance on a rug before he spoke again.

"This isn't a tent; it's a garden; it's an oasis. I came to make a deal. One live camel with a week's supply of figs and dates and water for one dead donkey—the one covered with all that fine linen. My mother had linen like that. She kept it for her daughters-in-law. Priceless. Just to keep the birds and the scorpions and the ants from the carcass of an ass?"

"You speak Hebrew well," Joseph said.

"My mother's tongue," the soldier explained. "My father is a Lebanese. He joined the tenth legion because he was hungry. He married my mother in Ramah. He taught me how to use the lance and the broadsword. And he taught me about the Roman gods. Maybe he was right. Maybe there is no Yahweh."

Joseph shook his head slowly.

"You did not become a Roman soldier because you believed in Mars or Jove. You, too, were hungry, son."

"Hungry and afraid. Like Moses, I saw a rich Gentile killing a Jew and I flung my lance through his fat red neck. I didn't have to pull it out of him. I just had to pick it up, a dozen steps behind his body. Then I fled to the Roman camp and demanded to be a soldier. They wouldn't take me at first. They said I was too young. But when they saw what I could do with the lance they were eager to have me and I was safe."

Mary came forward, her face twitching with agony—a line of scripture singing a cruel lament in her mind. "A voices is heard in Ramah. Rachel is weeping for her children and will not be consoled, for they are no more."

"Ramah?" she said to the soldier. "Your mother is in Ramah?"

"Lady," the soldier cried, "forgive me. I did not see you. And then, just for a moment, I thought you were my mother herself. But you are so young! And so—so very beautiful! Yes, Ramah and Bethlehem, all the little villages around Jerusalem.

"We go there now lest there be an uprising among the people against King Herod. We must move swiftly. If your donkey hadn't died we would have had to slaughter and eat my camel. Did you ever eat camel meat? Roasted or grilled or raw? A roasted ass will be a banquet! We are starving, lady, and desperate. A hungry army riding into battle never rides back."

"But you will not eat my faithful little friend," Joseph shouted. "He is more than an ass. He is almost human. He is the only beast that ever carried the son of Yahweh and his mother. He is the only beast who ever heard the halleluiahs of the angels. He is the only . . . "

"So that's who you are," the soldier interrupted, falling on his knees. "You are the people the murderous Herod is looking for! You are still in frightful danger. But my camel, even though she limps, may save you. There is a caravan of Herod's men not far away. I talked to one of them about the massacre. I am sure my mother had many children after I ran away and I know that one was almost two years old."

Mary was walking up and down, up and down, holding

the baby close to her. Sorrow, terrible sorrow in her eyes, but no tears.

"You talked to him?" she asked. "You did not hate him?"

The soldier was confused. "I don't know. He was drunk. All of them were drunk.

"Once when I was a little boy I lay on the grass and looked up at the clouds and I wished I was as unanchored and as free as they were so that I could go where I wanted to and see every part of the world. Then I learned that the clouds weren't free at all. They were slaves to the winds. We are all slaves, especially soldiers. We do what we are told to do. We cut a baby in half or swing it around and smash its head against a wall. Then we go somewhere and drink so that we can forget. No, I did not hate the soldier. I hated Yahweh!

"If we are his chosen people why does he let a mad king butcher us?"

"Why did he kill Joseph's donkey?" Mary asked. "Why did he cripple your camel? Who dares ask God why? Why did he let the children die? Those holy little innocents! Maybe he wanted them in heaven. Why not? Didn't his son shed his blood for them? Those few drops of blood at his circumcision could have redeemed the world! A million billion worlds!

"Martyrdom! The choicest jewel heaven can give! They are the first to go to heaven. The very first! And Ramah will be comforted in the Lord's own time."

In my dream or meditation or whatever it was, I was surprised at this line the angels had written for Mary. I had always thought that the good thief on the cross was the first to go to heaven. But then, who am I to argue about such things? (Pardon the interruption; let the play go on).

The baby leaned forward and touched the soldier's hand. And he made some sort of sound. Mary thought it was a cough. Joseph thought it was a sneeze. But the soldier knew what it was and he kissed the baby's finger.

"It is my Roman name," he said. "I was Abou Raya Said, an impossible name for a Roman legionary. Now I am Longinus! And I shall be a Tribune!"

The agony softened for a moment in Mary's eyes.

"You will be greater than that," she said. "You shall be a centurion, and even more. My son has chosen you."

"Then it's a deal," the soldier said abruptly coming back to business; and as abruptly leaving business entirely alone. "Did you ever see fire on a black night burning under the carcass of a donkey? Flames laughing at the soldiers who turn it gently so it will not burn and at all the soldiers standing around and trying not to snatch a piece of meat while it is still cooking? Did you ever listen to the juices dripping into the pans arranged along the sides of the fire?"

"I have some herbs for you," Mary said. "Now ask why the Lord made me bring such things along."

"And I have a skin of wine," Joseph said. "For flavor! Why did I bring it? So I could help the angels cook my old friend for your banquet?"

Perplexity returned to the legionary's face.

"But if the child is really the son of God why do you have to hide from Herod or anyone else on earth? If he be the son of God he can never be hurt. He can never die."

"No," Mary corrected him gently. "He came on earth so that he might die. As the ass died and as the children died.

"You will see him die, Centurion Longinus. And then you will know all the answers.

"Your name will never die. You will wear a robe such as not even Solomon in all his glory ever owned. And your lance will do more than the rod of Joseph. It will touch a rock—a rock rejected by the builders—and bring living water gushing out of it so long as the world endures. And it will bring wealth unheard of to all the people of the world!"

Joseph picked up the bells and went outside the tent. He put them on the camel. The beast arose in her clumsy way and walked around the tent to show she was no longer lame.

"The Archangel Michael sent you," Joseph whispered to her, "so I'll call you Michaela."

The animal nodded her silly head and jingled the silver bells. To Joseph the music still had the echoes of the angel's halleluiahs! He put on his hat, raised his head to the Lord, and said a silent prayer.

CHAPTER 19

JESUS AND TOBIAS: TWO DIVINE ERRANDS

Sometime between two and three o'clock in the morning on the feast of St. Anthony, June 13th, I heard someone knocking on my desert window, the one that looks to heaven. It startled me. No one ever did that before. Not even the tallest man standing on the tallest camel could reach that window. No one was throwing stones. Someone was knocking, knocking, knocking. A voice spoke to me. It wasn't St. Anthony or anybody speaking aloud. Maybe it was my own imagination. It said: "Get up. Turn on the lights. Put on your bathrobe. Get paper and pen and write." I got up immediately, put on my bathrobe, found a pen, ripped an envelope open and wrote on the back of it. I didn't know what I was writing at first. But words came easily. "The Holy Spirit escorted the Son of God into the immaculate womb of Mary just as the angel Raphael guided Tobias, the son of Tobit, on his journey.

"Christ, like Tobias, was going on an errand to collect a debt for his father and to win himself a bride, the most beautiful bride in the world, the Church. The angel Raphael guided Tobias with great honor and success. The Holy Spirit guided the child into the virgin womb and her womb became fertile with the fertility of God himself. Christ is the only man born of woman who had no earthly father. Mary is the only woman entirely possessed by God, the only woman ever entirely to possess God. Christ was God when he mysteriously and miraculously entered her womb. Mary was the first cathedral, the first basilica, the first tabernacle of the Lord. He was God and he reigned in her during all her pregnancy. He was God when he found his way into the cave at Bethlehem. His coming and going was as incomprehensible as his coming into the room that had been locked against him. All the doors had been closed and locked and all the windows had been shut and Christ suddenly appeared in the room."

I put down the pencil and went back to bed. In the morning I picked up the Bible and looked for the story of Tobias and the angel Raphael. Like so many stories in the Old Testament, it is a foretelling, a sort of prophecy of the adventures of Jesus.

Tobit, the father of Tobias, had been blinded by the droppings of birds and his eyes were full of cataracts. In his old age he remembered that he had entrusted some money—a vast sum—to a friend living far away. So he sent Tobias not only to collect the money but also to marry the beautiful Sarah, one of his near kin. The angel Raphael appeared to Tobit in the guise of an ordinary man and offered to escort the boy on his travels. Tobit liked the angel and agreed.

On their way to the far country the two travelers found a great fish, some of which they ate and some of which they salted and carried away with them to eat later. They also took the gall, the liver, and the heart of the fish at the angel's insistence.

The angel Raphael really arranged the marriage for Tobias telling him how beautiful the maiden was, how tragic her story and how wonderful her family was. Seven times Sarah had been married. Seven times the bridegroom fell dead as he approached the bridal chamber. "There is a devil, Asmodeus, who is in love with Sarah," the angel said.

"And he kills the bridegroom before he can claim his bride." Tobias almost rejected the idea of marrying the girl, not because he was afraid of dying but because he was the only son of his parents and they would grieve most horribly for him and he would fail in his errand to return with the money and the bride.

But when he saw the girl nothing mattered. He must marry her that night.

"Throw the heart and the liver of the fish on the embers of the fire in the bridal chamber," the angel advised, "and the smoke of its incense will chase the devil into Egypt and he will never come back and you will not die."

How many Christians know that the first sign that Christians gave each other was not the sign of the cross but the sign of the fish? The Greek word for fish is spelled with letters whose initials stand for: "Jesus Christ, Son of God, Savior."

A man sat on a rock and drew a curved line in the sand. Many men passed him. Perhaps someone would complete the sign and then they would talk of God and perhaps a community of Christians and someone would consecrate bread and wine and there would be a feast.

Throwing the heart and the liver of the fish into the embers was like throwing your hope and faith in the sacred heart of Christ, thus making yourself immune to the malice of the devil.

I thought, too, as I read the book that Sarah was the symbol, not only of Mary of Nazareth, Our Lady of the Seven Dolors, but also of Mary Magdalen who once was possessed of seven devils.

I liked the way Tobias came home. He spent two weeks feasting with his father-in-law while his parents were frantic with worry waiting for him to return.

When he returned he and the angel hurried ahead of all the people he was bringing with him. His father-in-law had given him half of all he owned: slaves, cattle, mules, horses, household goods. It made a tremendous procession. Tobias and the angel went ahead and were warmly embraced by his mother. The gall of the fish he rubbed on his father's eyes and the cataracts fell from them one by one, and Tobit could see again.

I thought of God the Father waiting impatiently for his son's return. The God of justice, the God of vengeance, the God of wrath, the God who would drown every living thing on earth except the people and the animals in the ark, the God who would drown the army of Pharaoh in the sea, the God who would burn the cities of Sodom and Gomorrah for the unnatural sins of their men, the God who would turn Lot's wife into a pillar of salt because she dared to disobey him and turn back as she and her husband were fleeing from the wicked cities.

Listen: This is God speaking; God befouled by the sins of man and blinded with divine wrath. Thus says the Lord:

> For three crimes of Israel, and for four
> I will not revoke my word,
> Because they sell the just man for silver
> And the poor man for a pair of sandals.
> They trample the heads of the weak into the dust of
> the earth
> And force the lowly out of the way.
> Upon garments taken in pledge they recline beside
> any altar;
> And the wine of those who have been fined they

drink in the house of their god.
Beware, I will crush you into the ground as a wagon
crushes when laden with sheaves.
Flight shall perish from the swift, and the strong
man shall not retain his strength;
The warrior shall not save his life, nor the bowman
stand his ground;
The swift of foot shall not escape, nor the horseman
save his life.
And the most stouthearted of warriors shall flee
naked on that day, says the Lord.

(Amos 2:6-8, 13-16)

I thought I could see Jesus rub his father's eyes with the
gall. Not the gall of the fish but the gall, the bitterness, the
grief of his passion and his death so that the cataracts of
vengeance and judgment and wrath fell away from the
divine eyes and he looked again on earth with pity and with
love.

CHAPTER 20

THE GARDEN GRAVEYARD

Between six and seven o'clock in the morning I woke in St. Michael's Hospital, Toronto, and heard a familiar voice yammering and yammering.

It was the sort of voice you do not hear with your ears but with your heart and mind and, I suppose, with your imagination. I was irritated at first because I wanted to go back to sleep and because I knew this voice would insist on telling me its story in its own way in spite of everything I could do to stop it.

A man learns more by listening than by thinking. Wisdom comes from the lips of other men, seldom from one's own lips. So I lay back and listened.

"The most gracious gardens grow from the graves of holy Jews."

I sat up. This might be interesting.

A nurse brought me breakfast. A nurse came in and took some blood out of my left arm. Another nurse came in and took some blood out of my other arm. A doctor with a beard came in and asked me a lot of questions. But the mysterious voice babbled on and on.

I tried to interrupt it several times.

"Did you know that eating a strawberry, ripe and sweet and dressed in a bridal gown of powdered sugar, can be as exhilarating and heartwarming as saying a Hail Mary?"

The voice ignored me.

"Do you know Dr. Callahan?" I asked.

The voice began to talk about some place called Zuni.

"Zuni," I asked. "Do you mean the Zuni Indians? Or are you trying to say Arizuni?"

Dr. Callahan is my doctor, my eye doctor. I don't know whether he has faith enough to move mountains but he can move a cataract without batting an eye.

"The city of Zuni," the voice said, "worshiped the sun as a god."

My private nurse came to give me a pill and to take my pulse. Another nurse came in to take my temperature. But nothing disturbed the voice.

It was coming through my desert window, the one that looks toward heaven, the stubborn one that always sticks no matter what I do to raise it.

You realize I had my traveling desert with me. I take it wherever I go as an oyster takes its shell—especially if the shell has a pearl in it. My desert is full of pearls and I have as little to do with their making as the oyster has with his.

The oyster gives up his pearl eventually. I put mine on paper.

Nothing disturbed or halted the voice. It talked slowly, leading up to some sort of climax.

This can be very annoying to an author who has to have the plot in his mind before he writes and who cannot bear waiting for some other author to finish what he has in mind. But I am a patient patient, so I listen, and this is the story that rewarded my patience:

The city of Zuni was ruled by the high priest of the Sun, a man of arrogance, avarice and ambition. He had about five or six hundred assistant priests and he owned what little army there was in the city. He allowed the army to loot and rape and kill; and he allowed the priests to do what they liked. The priests and the soldiers lived on the fat of the land. The citizens lived on the bones.

Now it happened that in this ancient city there was a man who knew all about soil—where palm trees would grow highest and give the best shade, where olive trees would ripen the quickest and flowers would grow most beautifully. He had traveled all over the earth studying soil, analyzing it, letting sand run through his hands, toying with dirt and with clay.

The high priest of Zuni thought so much of him that he decided to make him king. He did away with his predecessor on some pretext or other and on a certain day in spring installed him with great pomp and splendor in the royal chair facing the flower beds that grew between him and the palace walls.

This flower bed was a magnificent stretch of ground and was shaped in a cross. Lovely tall flowers grew there in solid clusters. They were all the bright colors of the earth. They made an incense that went all the way up to heaven.

The new king took his seat and he waved his hands to the crowd to be silent. Then he stood up and said: "Citizens of Zuni, I have been all over the earth looking for flowers like these and examining the soils in which they grew. I have never seen such beautiful flowers although I have seen the same species. They don't grow in soil like this. No flowers such as these should grow here at all except for one reason.

"This is the graveyard of the Jews. You will remember that years ago when there was a solar eclipse our city rose in panic and cried out that the God of the Jews had profaned the sanctity of the sun and we decreed that all Jews must die.

"We were barbarians then. We didn't know about such

things as an eclipse, that the sun's light could be hidden by the shadow of the moon.

"We murdered the Jews and laid them here. But the God of the Jews has honored their graves with these beautiful flowers."

He started to sit down but he lurched and fell to the ground with an arrow in his heart fired by the chief priest of Zuni, the priest of the god of the Sun.

The voice stopped for a moment. "He blasphemed," the priest explained, "so he had to die."

"The king is dead, long live the king."

He placed his hand on the boy who knelt beside him. "You are now the king of Zuni," he said. "I give you my allegiance. Always remember it was I who taught you everything you know. And it is I who make you king!"

"I will remember," the boy said. "Hear my first command. My father's body will be laid here in the center of the cross of flowers. His heart was with the Jews. Let his body rest there also."

The new king turned then and ran to his room like a little boy, perhaps to weep, perhaps not, I don't know.

The priests of Zuni cut down all the flowers that grew on the graves of the Jews and put them in the furnace.

The new king had powerful weapons given him by the priest. One was cunning. Cunning is sharper and deadlier than poison. And he had guile which is more dangerous than famine, plague, flood, fire or massacre.

And he ruled the high priest with these weapons. He would come to the priest at times with a very thoughtful face and say such things as these: "I have been thinking over what you said, great priest, and I know now that you were right. I thought at first it was the wine talking in you, now I know it was the wisdom of your god. The chief assistant priests you mentioned, the ones you thought were your enemies, really are your enemies.

"And I think you are merciful in sending them into exile—and you were right all the time. The soldiers who rob the people, they should be sold as slaves. And the money they bring should be given to the people who were robbed and to the treasury you control.

"And you were, of course, right in thinking that the soldiers who rape should be turned into eunuchs and sold to the harem masters, not to work in the harems but in the stables. And the soldiers who kill the people of Zuni should be given as slaves to their nearest of kin."

In this way the king weakened the priesthood and the army. Meanwhile he recruited soldiers of his own and paid them out of his private purse.

Seasons passed and it was summer. He called a synod of the priests and noble citizens to meet him between the palace and the city walls.

Flowers had begun to grow again over the graves. Over his father's grave grew a mass of beautiful small flowers that perfumed the air more beautifully than the whole garden had done the previous year.

On one side of the courtyard weeds grew on the graves of those priests the king had marked for punishment and whom the high priest had sent into eternal exile.

The king said: "Today the sun god desires to reward each of his priests with a golden silken cord around his neck and the high priest with a collar of gold."

The idea had come to him from one of the diaries left by his father which concerned a priest of the Jews, Elias, who slew all the priests of a god named Baal. When he finished speaking he raised his arm.

Immediately the soldier standing behind each priest dropped the cord over each shaven head and tightened it around each fat, red neck. The corporal of the guard adjusted the collar of gold around the neck of the high priest.

The king raised his hand again—this time as though he were saying goodbye. And the soldiers tightened the cords until all the priests were dead.

The king rose and stood over the body of the high priest. "You lived for gold," he said. "It is fitting to die by gold. I will have you and all your priests buried over there in the weeds like the priests of Baal.

"And we shall send one of our courtiers to the king of the Jews and ask him for a priest who will come and tell us why such lovely flowers grow from the bones of pious Jews. Also why the flowers always take the shape of a cross.

"The Jews were not buried in a cruciform grave. They were buried in a deep moat, hundreds piled on hundreds. And the moat was filled with lime and sand and dirt and rubble of all kinds.

"I want to know why the flowers grow from this moat in the shape of a cross."

The voice was still talking as I was put on a stretcher and carried into the operating room. I might have been talking while I was being uncataracted. I don't know. I don't know anything.

Sometime later in the day I woke in my bed feeling very happy and wondering about my friend, the voice.

I think I knew what he was trying to tell me.

The Old Testament is filled with stories that are as

beautiful as the most beautiful of gardens!

And every flower-bed is shaped in the sign of the cross!

But nobody had to tell me that. And nobody had to explain about their shape. Both of us, you and I, know that everything in the Old Testament leads to Calvary.

CHAPTER 21

CHRISTMAS, 1974

The voice came through the upstairs window of my flexible desert—yes, the window still sticks—and woke me from a nervous sleep.

"Wake up, Groucho," it said, "and listen."

I woke up and reached for the light, put on my glasses, drank a glass of water, took my pills, and prepared to listen.

"What are you going to give your friends for Christmas?"

"I will say mass for them, of course, maybe all three of my Christmas masses. I will send out my usual Christmas card and I will wish every one of them a long life of peace and love."

"Is that all?" the voice asked. "Why don't you send every one of them a Bible?" I put out the light. Bibles! How was I going to buy a Bible for everybody? If I stole one from every motel and hotel in Canada and the United States I wouldn't have enough!

So I thought, maybe I could advise my friends to advise their friends to invest in this unique Christmas present.

In the U.S.A., where Christ is not allowed to enter the schoolroom, the book could be sent to the boy or girl in a plain brown or white innocent-looking envelope with no publisher's name on it. No teacher, no school principal, no member of the board of education, looking at such a package would guess its guilty secret. A boy or girl could be warned privately or by letter to hide the book in the dust jacket of some sexy bestseller and could read it anywhere without attracting the least attention.

The more I thought about this idea, the better I liked it.

There was a time when both Canadians and Americans used to boast with fatuous pride: "This is God's country."

We love the name of God in the United States. We put it proudly on our coins, "In God We Trust," and sent the coins circling through the world.

Alas, that was years ago. His name seldom passes from lip to lip these days. It passes only from greasy thumb to greasy thumb. And the greasy thumb always covers the name of God. However, the holy name remains on the coin.

They have taken the name from our public schools. When will they take it from the coins?

The Bible has two parts, the Old Testament and the New. It can be obtained as a single book or as two books. A young boy or a young girl will find the choicest literature in the world in the Old Testament. And more stories about violence, rape, incest, massacre, fraud, war and, depravity than in any of the pornographic books now on the market. (It is quite possible that most of our sexy authors get their plots out of this beautiful Old Testament). However, the stories in the Bible do not glorify either sin or sinners as our modern authors do.

The young readers will also find predictions about a new kingdom that is to come and a king who shall rule it and possess it forever.

He will be born of a virgin.

He will be the son of God.

He will be the savior of mankind.

This edition, unlike most books, has a very happy

beginning and it can have a happy ending only when the new edition has been digested.

There are many young groups in North America today who are trying to help this lost generation to find its way to peace and even to joy. I wish there were more.

Jesus is a powerful drug, habit-forming, stronger than opium and more powerful than whiskey or gin or wine or any liquor.

And Christmas is his birthday!

Maybe, Friends, I am like Martha, worried about too many things—inflation, pollution, job shortage, abortion, the population explosion, and our plans for permanent peace.

The Bible in the hands of our children would stop us from worrying about lack of oil and energy. It would make the whole world walk with confidence on the waters of God's love and care. It would reduce the crimes in our big cities. It might eliminate inflation and take care of all the poor in the way God wants them taken care of—not by alms but by love.

Of course, the objections to this man, Jesus, felt by the educators and some of our Supreme Court Justices may or may not have been born of the fact that Jesus had something of a police record. He was never convicted of any crime but he was legally condemned, tortured and duly executed by the law.

He was a man who loved the poor and the sinful more than he loved the righteous and the rich.

He often said that he loved sinners and he came to serve sinners and many sinners loved him. It may also be confessed that millions of his followers have been legally put to death because of their love for him.

Once he changed the whole world. He may do it again if people came to love each other. And perhaps that is what the world is afraid of.

Christmas at Madonna House promises to be a most glorious one.

It will be especially glorious to me because of a new Greek-Catholic chasuble that the people of Madonna House are making for me.

It will be a beautiful shade of red. It will be all wool and more than a yard wide. A staff worker, Tom Egan in Regina, Saskatchewan, wove the cloth for me and Gisele Branchaud is cutting it up for me. One night months ago here in my Combermere desert I dreamed of this particular vestment.

I dreamed of decorating the front of it with a beautiful picture of Our Lady of Guadalupe, "a woman clothed with the sun and the moon beneath her feet." The next morning I told somebody of this dream and learned that Patti Birdsong was embroidering just such a picture. It was a startling coincidence. I saw Patti and she said, "I will embroider it for you."

I mentioned all this to Father Callahan, the director general of our priests. He suggested I put a rose on the shoulder to implement the story of Juan Diego who, as most everybody knows, found roses on top of a mountain in Mexico in mid-December when he saw the Blessed Virgin and heard her voice, sweeter than all the sounds of the earth.

While I was thinking of this, another one of our staff

workers, Rochelle Greenwood, asked if she could embroider the rose for me. I was delighted. "Make it a yellow rose," I said, "in honor of the Little Flower, St. Therese."

When Catherine was nursing people in Combermere in the early days, especially winter when doctors could never get into the bush because of all the snow and ice on the roads, Catherine always left two nurses with the patient. One was Our Lady and the other was the Little Flower! Catherine never lost a patient.

While we were talking about this vestment one day, Mary Kay Rowland who has spent some years in Haifa, Israel, as secretary to Archbishop Raya, volunteered to decorate the rear of the chasuble with a yellow Byzantine cross.

The vestment will be completed before Christmas and I shall probably wear it for my three masses on Christmas day.

It might even be done by the feast of Our Lady of Guadalupe!

Many people have written me letters about my health or lack of health. Some are wondering what I am going to do about walking upstairs.

Madonna House has solved that problem for me. They have put a moving chair on the stairway leading from the dining room to our chapel. I sit in the chair, put my finger on a button, and go up or down without any trouble at all. God is good!

CHAPTER 22

FIRST VISIT TO COMBERMERE

A few days ago everybody in Madonna House here in Combermere rushed into my flexible and yielding little desert. The place expanded and became an auditorium; and a number of Canadians, men and women staff workers expressed in poetry and prose their love and admiration for Canada.

I was moved and impressed.

Some days later Catherine herself told her ideas and her love for this great country which had taken her, a refugee from Red Russia so many years ago, and has treated her so wonderfully for the last twenty-odd years. When Catherine had gone and the crowd of staff workers had followed her, I stayed in my desert for a while looking through the back window—the one that does not stick—seeing Canada as I saw it on my first trip to Combermere in 1945.

I saw again the railroad train that took us from Ottawa to Barry's Bay. I saw for the first time one of the loveliest countries in all the world. I opened the train window. "Canada," I said to Catherine, "smells a lot like Wisconsin!"

I used to visit Wisconsin when I was very young and I loved the country. It had something Canada lacked however, the smell of wood smoke.

It had a railroad just like this one that dallied at every station along its way and took its time to reach its destination.

"And once," I said, "once when that old train stopped

for no reason at all—like this train does—I saw a blue flower. One little blue flower! It was across the tracks and you won't believe it, but I was tempted to jump out the window, pick the posy, and get back in. I dared myself to do it. But suddenly the train started up.

"Honestly, I could hardly contain myself. That flower meant so much to me. I couldn't understand it!"

"What on earth are you talking about?" she said.

"The blue of your eyes," I said.

"Oh. Well, they've always been blue."

"I've noticed that," I said, ending the conversation but still remembering the forlorn unpicked flower on the Kickapoo right-of-way forty years and more ago!

Two living blue eyes are worth more than two million just-remembered flowers. (But why argue about it with your wife?)

Our train stopped at many places and stayed there until it made sure it was ready to proceed. Every depot, I thought, was the front parlor of its town and the people were all guests at a party. They looked hearty and more than a little friendly.

These people seemed to be my kind of people.

I had a bad moment when the train stopped at Barry's Bay and I saw the shabby little wooden depot. It was painted the color of stale chocolate or overdone liver.

"Isn't it wonderful?" Catherine cried. "That's John in the Model T. He's going to take us to the house."

"Why can't we call a cab?" I asked.

She laughed.

"No taxis between here and Ottawa," she said. "If we don't go with John we'll have to wait for the mailman and he won't leave for Combermere until late this afternoon."

"In a mail truck! Rural free delivery! Who's John?"

She left me to talk and laugh with the station agent and his assistant. I talked to John. Rather he talked to me.

"You for the Cubs or Sox?"

"I used to be a Cub fan," I admitted.

"Maybe when the Cubs were good, huh? Now you're off 'em?"

"Yep."

He was such a likable boy I almost helped him put the luggage into the car.

I found out later he was the son of a neighbor. He had driven thirty miles out of his way and waited two hours to give us a lift from Barry's Bay to the house in Combermere—a house Catherine said was really a modern palace.

I wondered if all Canadian neighbors were like that.

In the days that followed I found that indeed they were.

The people in our community were of all kinds: German, French, Polish, Slavic, Irish, Scotch, and English. No Swedes. I was sorry about that.

We had had plenty of Swedes in our neighborhood in Chicago when I was growing up. They were an unceasing delight to me. I got acquainted with boys and girls by going close to one of their houses to sing my battle cry: "Ten thousand Swedes came through the weeds, to lick one sick Norwegian."

And ah!—the black eyes! And oh!—the bloody noises that battle cry produced! I knew the *Touch Of Sweden* long before somebody thought of putting it into a bottle.

I loved those Swedes, fighting the boys and kissing the girls; but I hadn't come to Canada to get acquainted with people.

I had come on a visit for two weeks, a vacation. I had come from Chicago. I had come reluctantly. I hated the country, or thought I did, and I never bothered about my neighbors. I didn't know the names of most of them.

Life to me at this time was unendurable outside big cities. I had no intention of staying in Combermere long enough to get hay seeds in my heart.

I just wanted to see the house that Catherine loved, go swimming in the Madawaska which she thought was the most beautiful river in the world, and maybe pick some blackberries in the woods.

So what happened?

So, sitting at the table in the main room of this bleak little house in the Canadian back-bush, I looked out at the majestic river and the tall pines and the beautiful maples and the brightness of birch trees. And I said aloud to my own amazement, "I am going to buy this house and live here."

That's what Canada does to a man!

In their talks in my expanded desert Catherine and all the staff workers talked about the peace they had found in Canada.

Canada, everyone concluded, was the most peaceful nation on the face of the earth. It had never started a war though it had fought in many. Its job was to keep the peace.

In Combermere in due time I too felt this great peace that Canada holds.

It really is a land of peace and beauty and wealth untold. Its neighbors are really the most helpful people in the world as we have learned during the last thirty years.

I feel more at home in Canada somehow than I do in the U.S.A. And I have no more hunger for the big cities.

I am not a Canadian citizen yet I feel that Canada is my real home and I don't want to live anyplace else.

Also I have to agree with Catherine and all our Canadian staff workers that the people of Canada are the friendliest people in the world. Except, of course, when they are playing hockey!

CHAPTER 23

THE MARIAN PRESS

My traveling desert bogged most happily down in Chicago on its way to Winslow, Arizona, and I became aware of one of the most amazing realities of my long and amazing life.

Two Madonna House staff workers accompanied me here to the home of my family and have enjoyed thoroughly the time we spent in this city. One of these is Dr. Carlos Miura, a Japanese who was born in Argentina and licensed as a physician in Canada. The other is a graduate nurse, a product of the Mayo Brothers Clinic in Rochester, Minnesota, Clare Becker. You wonder how people like these get into Madonna House. Why they give up all ambitions—why they make vows to live in poverty, chastity, and obedience. But there are no answers. There are more than a hundred others like them back home in Combermere and in various parts of the world.

We flew from Toronto and arrived without incident worthy of mention, but the next morning I could hardly get out of bed. My stomach plumbing was in terrible disarray or disarrangement or dissatisfaction—whatever the right word is, and the doctor and the nurse worked over me all day long. Carlos found a candle of Our Lady of Guadalupe. He lighted it with glee and put it beside my bedside. The nurse hung my new chasuble against the window on the other side, the red chasuble with the beautiful picture of Our Lady of Guadalupe showing on the front. Dr. Carlos sang bits of Spanish and American songs and parts of the

Byzantine liturgy while he worked on me, but he sang only in the morning, in the afternoon, and in the evening. Midnight was as quiet as the death watch. For three days my stomach plumbing bothered me but something else bothered me even more. That was why I was suffering like this and yet feeling happy about it. Did Our Lady have some particular reason for sending me this particular gift or was I just imagining things? Eventually I came to the conclusion that she was trying to tell me something and I began to ask her what it was. She let me know simply that I had underrated my two sisters and my brother and that they were very great in her eyes.

I have known each of these three for over fifty years and never before had it occurred to me that they were half so great as they are. You know how it is with a big brother. "This is my sister Kathleen—this is my sister Eileen. Cute, huh? And intelligent. They are fighting off the boys because each wants to help Mom in her old age.

"This is my brother Tom. He thinks he can lick anyone in the world, and maybe he can. He and my brother Bill, the youngest in the family, are really men of might. They are both newspapermen. They work on different newspapers but sometimes they meet on the same story, as they did on one memorable occasion when an official, a sort of police chief, ordered them out of one of the big wholesale houses in Chicago. Bill picked the man up and threw him to Tom, saying, 'I don't like him nor his language, you keep him.' Tom replied, 'I don't want him either. Take him back.' They threw him from one to another five or six times in a good-natured way, put him tenderly down, brushed him off, assured him that anger hurt only the angry and chided him for his piteous use of profanity. 'It has neither heights nor depths,' says Bill, 'nor color nor imagination.' 'And it's vulgar,' Tom said, 'and very disturbing to good humor.' "

Now, because of a hip injury, Tom walks sometimes with one cane, sometimes with two, sometimes with a pair of crutches. He works as a public relations man for an automatic electric firm many miles away from home. He has to get up at six in the morning to get to work on time and he seldom gets home before six in the evening. Usually my sister Kathleen goes to the window overlooking the street about five-thirty and begins to watch for him. Tom has never smoked and has never drunk anything with alcohol in it. He has never used narcotics and he has never married.

My sister Kathleen is a retired court reporter with at least two bad knees and various and sundry pangs of arthritis but she goes where she wills, when she wills, and as she wills.

My sister Eileen is an ex-schoolteacher who believes that every public school became a jungle as soon as God was taken out of it by the law. She was glad to retire when she could. She and Kathleen and Tom, I learned to my utter stupefaction, are the doggonest, stubbornest, most devoted, most courageous and most self-giving missionaries in North America.

It was worth all the agony of my stomach to learn this profound truth. Between them they have organized, incorporated, and operated an apostolate called the Marian Press for the last twenty years.

I used to look on this thing as a sort of family hobby and

now I see it takes real missionaries to make it click.

These three people are not missionaries in the ordinary sense of the word. They do not teach catechism; they do not hold prayer meetings; they do not write or preach. They know as little about the charismatic movement as I do. They do not work any miracles.

I take that back. The girls do work miracles with hams and spareribs and custard and apple pie and salad and things like that, but who would hold that against them?

The Marian Press begs, buys, collects, or in some way acquires all the Catholic books, magazines, pamphlets, and holy pictures they can possibly obtain and sends them by mail to many parts of the world. It sends practically two hundred or more parcels every month to missionaries, convents, leprosaria, hospitals, jails, and refugee camps. The cost in postage is always somewhere between two hundred and three hundred dollars a month. There is very little money donated to this mission so my sisters and my brother dig into their pensions or their pocket money to pay the bills, and the postage goes up and up.

Lately a lot of Catholic magazines have gone out of business and those still published have become expensive to send abroad. They are too full of ads so Eileen made a plea to the *New World*, a Catholic paper printed in and for the Chicago diocese, asking for fresh supplies of magazines and books. This is when I began to learn how great these people are. Men like me write with divine help about God and his mother and the saints, print it in a magazine or book, and forget it. Somebody may read it; somebody may not. It doesn't matter much to us who write. Incidentally, most of us who write of God write for priests and nuns and really fervent Catholics; but my kid sisters and my kid brother put the "good news" into the hands of dying murderers and prostitutes and thieves and lepers and hungry refugees.

I wonder how many thieves went from the fall-away hospitals up to heaven after reading the Catholic literature that my brother and sisters worked so hard to get to them. It should be as easy to go to heaven from a soft pillow in the hospital as from a hard pillow of the cross on Calvary. It should be as easy for the strumpet to weep tears of remorse and love as it was for the Magdalene.

It is one thing to teach or preach; it is quite another thing to put the message in the sinners' hands.

My sisters and my brother have had much opposition in their apostolate. Some of it in a peculiar kind of way from the United States post office. A few days ago a postman brought back two packages which the Marian Press had sent to an island in the South Pacific. The missionary had died and nobody wanted the magazines and books that had been sent from Chicago. "I've come to collect," the postman said, "two dollars and sixteen cents for each parcel. It took that much to send it and it takes that much to bring it back."

"But I didn't ask to have it sent back," Eileen said, "and I don't want it back, take it away."

"If I take it back," the postman said, "it will go into the dead letter office."

"O.K.," Eileen said, "and some day there will be a resurrection and Catholic literature will live again even in the dead letter office and it may do a lot of good!"

I went to Arizona with great joy when the time came to go, having learned at last how really great my people are.

CHAPTER 24

THE VANISHING OF MY GREY DAYS

The Lord has put a grey day around my little desert here in Arizona and grey days are given to a man so that he may think.

This is not one of his grade A grey days nor one of his Z's, but it is grey enough not only for thought, but also for wonder.

Why am I lying here in bed in pain when I should be out hunting petrified wood or visiting old friends? Why am I wearing the dunce cap for the whole school? In the old days, you know, when the schoolmaster discovered some nuisance had been committed in the classroom during one of his temporary absences, he asked the young scoundrel to indict himself. Usually nobody talked. That made the master single out someone he thought guilty and sit him on a stool in a corner with a dunce cap on his head.

That was a long, long time ago. A teacher who tried that today in any American school would undoubtedly be mobbed by the students. Teaching school has become a dangerous occupation.

Why was I wearing this dunce cap of pain?

I had left Combermere in fairly good health. My right arm had almost entirely recovered from its myositis infection and I thought I could go to my desert in Winslow, Arizona, without help. But higher authorities insisted it be otherwise. We got to Chicago in good shape and I went almost immediately into medical care. Again I was comforted that I could carry on by myself and for a few days in Winslow I did.

I said mass every morning for a week or so in the glory and beauty of my new chasuble with the picture of Our Lady of Guadalupe emblazoned on its front. It increased the congregation gradually every day.

Then one morning I was unable to get out of bed. The myositis had gone from the arm into the right leg. The divine master had picked me out as the one to wear the fool's cap and sit in a corner.

But somehow I couldn't worry about myself as much as I wanted to for I kept looking through the back window of my desert at my very odd past. I am a pauper, a beggar. I own nothing. I walk on the waters of God's providence. So how come I had brought with me from Canada my own private physician and my own private nurse?

I don't think the richest man in the world could buy for his personal use such wonderful and friendly people. I pay them nothing. They work for me twenty-four hours a day. And I mean they really work. If I wake at three o'clock in the morning coughing, the doctor comes quietly into my room. If I wake in the morning and find a glass of ice water close to my hand, then I know the nurse has been there and is waiting for me to get up.

Looking out that back window I see myself and Catherine taking a vow of poverty more than thirty years ago and I see all kinds of surprises springing from that action.

For instance, Doctor Miura, whom I have mentioned before, is young, a bachelor, a skilled physician, and one of our most devout staff workers. It is seemingly an accident that he became a Catholic. It is not an accident that he became such a fervent Catholic as he is.

"One day," says Carlos, "a bunch of us kids were playing in a field near our home. A man in a big truck drove up and gathered us all into the vehicle 'You are all going to be baptized,' he said. 'You are all going to be Holy Roman Catholics.'

"The Japanese, when they settle in other countries, usually adopt the laws and customs and religions of their neighbors so it was natural that we should become Roman Catholics. I was curious about this new faith and began to ask questions and to study it and to like it more and more."

Carlos learned English when he came to the U.S.A. to study medicine. In Cleveland, Ohio, he found a friend who told him about Madonna House. He came to Madonna House on a sort of exploration trip and decided that this was the life he wanted to live.

The nurse, Miss Clare Becker from Minnesota, is a graduate of Mayo Clinic who also came to Madonna House at the suggestion of a friend. She has served the apostolate in Virginia, in the West Indies, and in Peru and Honduras where she has gathered an extensive knowledge of Spanish. So she and Carlos talk and sing in Spanish as well as English all the day long and sometime play the guitar. Meanwhile, when he isn't attending me, Carlos walks around the neighborhood or adjusts matters in the house, fixes gates, and does other maintenance jobs.

There were four women regularly assigned to Madonna House in Winslow in 1974. Theresa Marsey, the local director, Kathy McVady, Miriam Stuhlberg, and Gay Doherty. The doctor looks after them, too, fending off colds and symptoms of flu and other diseases.

These girls also sing morning, noon and night. The place

is one of joyous hymns and laughter. So why am I left out of it?

Oddly enough I am not left out. I feel as joyous as they do, which is crazy, isn't it? While I write, the sun breaks through a cloud and a figure passes before the window that looks on Galilee and Judea and all the places ever visited by Christ, and I can see not too plainly a man staggering along wearing a fool's cap of thorns. He wears it like a crown, as though he were born to it, as though it conferred great privileges upon him, such as the privilege of atoning for all the sins of the world.

Slowly the greyness vanishes from my desert windows and the sun shines all around and I hear my doctor and my nurse singing together the Spanish hymn "Paloma Blanca."

I do not expect to remain in bed much longer. I think every day I get a little stronger and my right hand is beginning to show some signs of life. At least I can endorse a check and say a rosary for you and all the other people in the world.